KNIT
TO
FIT

By Sharon Brant
Edited by Kate Haxell

Q
QUAIL

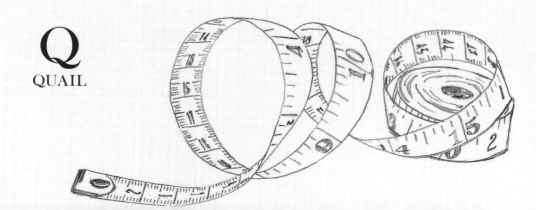

KNIT TO FIT
by Sharon Brant

First published in Great Britain in 2013
by Quail Publishing
www.quailpublishing.co.uk

Creative Direction: Darren Brant
Illustration: Lauren Bishop
Editor: Kate Haxell

British Library Cataloguing in Publication
Data. A catalogue record of this book is
available from the British Library.

ISBN 978-0-9567851-7-6

Printed in the United Kingdom by
CPI Colour Limited

CONTENTS

'IT'S ALL
IN THE
PLANNING.'

SHARON BRANT

INTRODUCTION

There are many positive aspects to knitting, and one of the most important is being able to make garments that perfectly suit and fit the person they are made for. Many people are put off knitting garments because they are not confident that, when they have finished weeks of knitting, the piece will fit and will look good. Why buy beautiful – and sometimes expensive – yarn, invest the next six weeks/months of your life in making something, and then have the disappointment of it not fitting well?

This book aims to change all of that for you. It will help you to understand your body shape, and which garment styles will suit that shape. It will show you how to work out the sometimes hidden measurements given in knitting patterns, and how they relate to your body. And, vitally, how you can adjust patterns to suit your shape and size. Please do read through all the chapters, rather than just jumping to pages you think you need, as this book is designed to be a complete fitting workshop.

In addition, there is a full library of body blocks to photocopy and use (see pages 87–94), plus a record card (see page 95) to get you into the good habit of making notes for every project you knit.

I hope that *Knit To Fit* will be every knitter's best companion.

Sharon x

Chapter 1
Understanding Body Shape

If you are going to invest time – and money – in knitting a garment, you need to know that when you have put the last stitch into it, you will feel happy and comfortable wearing it; then it is a success. Therefore, it is important to know which garment shapes suit you, and in order to do that you will need to know which body shape you are.

In this chapter I will describe and illustrate different body shapes, and discuss the key things to look out for when choosing garments to suit those shapes. Following these shape rules doesn't mean forfeiting personal style: 'rules' are there to be broken if you wish.

This process may mean you have to get the tape measure out and measure your body! Plus, it is always useful to stand in front of your wardrobe and try on lots of garments to help you really think about what suits you (see page 19).

When I talk about a fitted garment, I don't mean 'tight-fitting'! A fitted garment is one with shape: it doesn't matter how big you are, a shaped garment is always more slimming than a large baggy garment. The shaping can be varied to suit the fit that you feel comfortable wearing.

The great thing about knitting is that you are creating a piece of cloth to fit your body and nobody else's. So, it is time to forget if you are a small, medium or large; this is about making your own personal body block that will let you make a properly fitting garment every time.

I hate the names we use to describe our shapes – pear, apple, athletic, hourglass, inverted triangle – but you need to know the shape you are, so let's get this bit done quickly and then we can move onto the next chapter! If you are not sure which shape you are, you will have to measure your hips, waist and shoulders.

| APPLE | PEAR | ATHLETIC | HOURGLASS | INVERTED TRIANGLE |

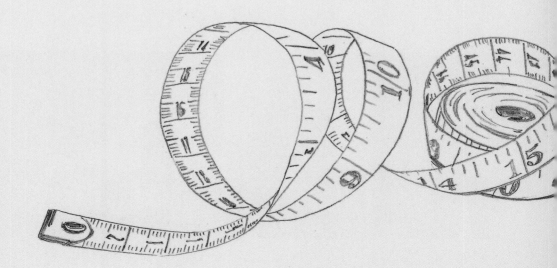

APPLE SHAPE

Your shoulders and hips are about the same measurement, and you have a tummy and bust. You need to hide your midriff so you look more like an apple core than an apple.

It is easy to think 'hide it all', and knit a long, baggy sweater, but actually shaped garments are good for apple figures. You need to make the most of your best body features, such as your cleavage and bottom.

GARMENT SHAPES AND FEATURES
Apple shapes should look for:

- V necklines and scooped necklines.
- Edge-to-edge jackets (jackets where the front edges do not overlap, or sometimes even touch), or single-button jackets.
- Fitted garments (don't panic at the thought of 'fitted', especially if you are plus-size: they take pounds off, trust me!).
- Well-fitting shoulders – not dropped shoulders – and fitted sleeves.

- Waterfall jackets (jackets that have a front neckline that drapes down over the bust and tummy area, and normally drapes lower than the bottom edge of the jacket).
- Wraparound cardigans (a patterned cardigan worn with a plain top underneath works well).

Boulevard, from Rowan brochure City Retreat.

Bute, from Rowan Magazine 52.

Frill, from Rowan brochure Studio 17.

Metropolitan, from Rowan brochure City Retreat.

PEAR SHAPE

Your shoulders are narrower than your hips. Pear shapes usually have a nice size bust and shoulders, but your hips and bum are what you need to think about.

The natural impulse is to hide your bottom, but actually the most flattering sweaters and cardigans are those that stop above your hips. And wearing fitted garments will make the most of your waist. You may have to change some of the shaping of a standard pattern, but that is why I am here and I will guide you through the changes you'll need to make (see pages 77–79).

GARMENT SHAPES AND FEATURES
Pear shapes should look for:

• Designs with shoulder detail, and you may want to knit some shoulder pads to broaden your shoulders a little. (Just subtle pads, we're not heading back to *Dallas* days!)
• Good shoulder and neck detail to attract the eye to the top half of your body.

• Shaped, short sweaters and cardigans.
• Belted cardigans are good, as are patterned garments.

Kintyre, from Rowan Magazine 52.

Whiting, from Rowan brochure Wintertide.

Dilys, from Rowan brochure Tweed.

Sauvignon, from Rowan brochure Parisian Nights.

ATHLETIC SHAPE

An athletic shape is straight up and down: your shoulders and hips are about the same measurement and you do not have much of a defined waistline. Athletic shapes usually have a smaller bust and a long body and arms.

The good news is that you can wear almost anything! However, avoid plunging necklines; an empire line is great for you. You can wear long-line jackets, which can be belted to create shaping. Fitted jackets and cardigans are good, but you need to look at the length of the body and the position of the shaping (see pages 66 and 77–79).

GARMENT SHAPES AND FEATURES

Athletic shapes should look for:

- Long-line sweaters and jackets, which can be belted.
- Fitted cardigans and sweaters.
- Wrapover cardigans.
- Knitted dresses and skirts.

Bliss, from Rowan *brochure* Easy Winter Nights.

Lidiya, from Rowan Magazine 48.

Martha, from Rowan *brochure* Studio 2.

Woolwich, from Rowan *brochure* Wintertide.

Hourglass Shape

Those with an hourglass figure have shoulders and hips that are about the same measurement, a curvy bust and a lovely nipped-in waistline. Fitted garments need to fit well; you may need to change the shaping to accentuate your waist (see pages 77–79). Also, make sure that there is enough ease so the garment doesn't pull around your hips or bust.

Use shoulder detail to emphasise your shape, and peplums are good to show off your hips.

Garment shapes and features

Hourglass shapes should look for:

- Edge-to-edge jackets (jackets where the front edges do not overlap; indeed, sometimes they don't even touch), or single-button jackets.
- Fitted garments (this doesn't mean tight-fitting, see page 8).
- Well-fitting shoulders – not dropped shoulders – and fitted sleeves.
- Waterfall jackets (jackets that have a front neckline that drapes down over the bust and tummy area, and normally drapes lower than the bottom edge of the jacket).
- Wrapover cardigans.
- Belted cardigans and jackets.
- Straight skirts.

Connie, from Rowan Magazine 50.

Glenda, from Rowan Magazine 50.

Headland, from Rowan brochure Cotton Classics.

Inga, from Rowan Magazine 48.

INVERTED TRIANGLE SHAPE

This sounds more like a mathematical question than a body shape: it means that your shoulders are wider than your hips, with usually a larger bust.

Broad shoulders are great for knitwear! You just need to balance out the other bits. Avoid boxy jackets and sweaters, and anything that has puffed or exaggerated shoulder detail.

GARMENT SHAPES AND FEATURES
Athletic shapes should look for:

- Asymmetric garments.
- Wrapover cardigans.
- Garments with long necklines.
- Waterfall necklines with ruffles (garments that have a front neckline that drapes down over the bust and tummy area, and normally drapes lower than the bottom edge of the jacket).

- Belted garments.
- Shaped garments.
- Long-line jackets and sweaters.

Ariadne, from Rowan brochure Seascapes.

Boston, from Rowan brochure Classic Casuals.

Martha, from Rowan Magazine 50.

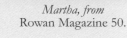

Paige, from Rowan Magazine 52.

YOUR STATURE

Once you have decided which shape you are, you also have to consider your height and how your body is proportioned. If you are tall, petite or a plus-size, this will affect which styles of garment suit you best.

PETITE

This doesn't just mean that you are short; petite people are particularly small-framed and often struggle with even the smallest size in a knitting pattern. Don't worry, I shall help you to make all the adjustments needed (see pages 62–81).

You need to avoid bulky yarns and fussy designs: take away details like pockets and frills and concentrate on good, simple shaping. Make sure you look out for the length of the body and where the waistline falls (see page 21). With fitted garments it is important to get the fit right – nothing should be baggy – and longer lines will make you look taller.

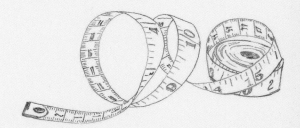

Cherish, from Rowan brochure Rowan Lace.

Harwood, from Rowan brochure Studio 2.

Selene, from Rowan brochure Seascapes.

Orkney, from Rowan Magazine 52.

TALL

The styles you choose if you are tall will depend on your body shape (see pages 10–14) as well as your height, but generally you will need to make sure you adjust a pattern to your own measurements and don't just go for a larger size because it will come out longer.

You need to understand your trunk length and leg length. I remember when I used to help my mum do the ironing and would iron my brother's jeans (what a good sister I was!!). He and I were the same height, but my jeans would hang off the end of the ironing board and my brother's didn't: I could always get his jeans on the ironing board, no problem!

A standard medium size may well perfectly fit one person who is 5' 5" tall, but their body could be a completely different length from that of someone else who measures the same height overall.

Keep to fairly simple knitwear designs, and wearing layers always helps to visually break your height down.

Tara, from Rowan Magazine 48.

Wight, from Rowan Magazine 52.

Humber, from Rowan Magazine 52.

Utsire, from Rowan Magazine 52.

PLUS SIZE

The important thing to remember if you are a plus size is that you still have a shape (see the shapes listed on pages 10–14), and that you should show it, though you can disguise the areas that protrude the most. Make sure the size you choose gives you enough ease: never wear anything that is too tight-fitting.

Follow the advice given for your shape, but it is important not to have dropped shoulders on garments. Also, make sure you don't choose bulky yarns or yarns that will stick to you: it sometimes helps to knit the yarn on a tight tension so that the fabric is less likely to stick.

Twisted Rib, from Knitting Goes Large.

Twisted Rib Cardigan, from Knitting Goes Large.

Houndstooth, from Classic Knits for Real Women.

Herringbone, from Classic Knits for Real Women.

DECIDING WHICH GARMENT TO KNIT

Now that you know which body shape you are and have an idea of what will suit your shape, it's time to decide what you want to knit. A good friend who will give you an honest opinion is an asset at this stage!

Go to your wardrobe and pull out all the types of garments that you would like to have a knitted version of: jackets, sweaters, shirts, dresses, skirts – they can be woven fabric or knitted. Try them on one at a time, and stand in front of the mirror. Look at each garment in detail and make notes – or ask a friend to write down – on what looks good, and what is not so good. Turn to pages 20–21 for some common fitting issues that you should look out for.

As well as the fit, this is also your opportunity to decide which garments you like the style of most, which are the most wearable, which would be more wearable if they were slightly different in some way, and what that difference might be. As you are going to be creating the new garments yourself, you can make all sorts of changes.

Hopefully you will find some garments that fit you well. However, don't reject garments that you love for their shape or style but that don't quite fit properly. In the next chapter I'll show you how to analyse a knitting pattern, and how to combine the results with the garment notes you've made to decide on the right pattern to knit for your body shape.

Do the shoulders fit properly? This can make a huge difference to your shape: well-fitting shoulders can make you look pounds lighter than ill-fitting ones will.

Do the sleeves fit correctly? Are they baggy under your arm? Remember that if a blouse in a fine fabric is baggy, when you knit the same shape the fabric will be bulkier, so a sleeve does need to fit properly.

Sweater fits badly on the shoulders.

Baggy sleeves and sleeve length is too long.

Are the sleeves the right length? Do you actually have one arm longer than the other? (This is quite common!)

Does the neckline suit you? Try on high necks and low necks, and as many different-shaped necklines as you can find: you will soon see which look best.

Is the length right? If a garment looks good in most ways, but you are unsure about the length, try folding up and pinning the hem at various different heights to see the effect.

Is the length right but the waistline is in the wrong place? There is little more annoying than wearing a fitted cardigan and having it keep riding up until you feel that the waistline is under your armpits!

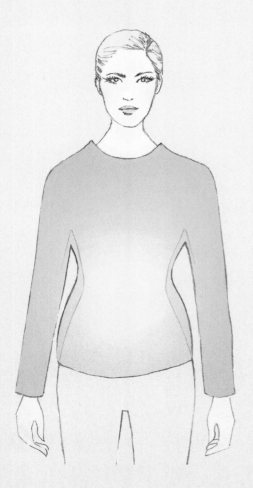

A garment of the correct length, but the shaping is in the wrong place.

Chapter 2

Choosing a Design to Suit Your Body Shape

So now you have an idea of which styles suit you and what you want to achieve by knitting a garment for yourself, all you have to do is look through a selection of knitting magazines and brochures and find the perfect sweater... Alright, I know that that isn't always so easy: do you have to turn the page past a sweater that you like for one reason, but it doesn't tick all the boxes for you? No you don't! If you like the body design but the sleeves are the wrong length, or the body is shaped and you don't like that, or perhaps the neckline is not right for you, I am going to help you fix all those problems and more!

Sometimes a garment is perfect in every way, then the only decision you need to make is which size to knit. When you go into a store you have to decide if you are a small, medium, large – and that varies from store to store. But when you are knitting your own garment, you don't have to decide on a conventional sizing, because you are going to make it to the measurements you require.

So start looking through magazines and find a design you like, one that really catches your eye. Maybe it is the shape, the stitch or the yarn it is knitted in that appeals. Write down what you like about it, and then what you don't. Don't forget to look at the line drawing that accompanies each knitting pattern; this will give you quite a lot of extra detail information that you may not be able to see in the photography.

Remember that when the designers make up sample garments for photography they don't know the exact measurements of the

model who will wear it: a model maybe
listed as wearing a size 10, but the designer
doesn't know her actual shoulder width, arm
measurement, etc. Most models are extremely
tall, so their bodies are much longer than
those of the majority of us. Also, the tricks of
the trade on photo shoots do involve safety
pins at the back in order to make the garment
look a great fit. These are all good reasons as
to why you should never rely on how a model
is wearing a garment. The important thing is
to decide why you like the item, and then see
what you can alter to make it right for you and
your shape.

A Rowan knitting pattern will have a photograph of the garment on a model, and a line drawing that shows clearly the shape of the piece. You may find that the (rather boring looking) drawing is as useful as the photograph in helping you decide whether or not to knit the garment.

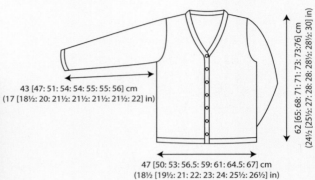

43 [47: 51: 54: 54: 55: 55: 56] cm
(17 [18½: 20: 21½: 21½: 21½: 21½: 22] in)

62 [65: 68: 71: 71: 73: 73:76] cm
(24½ [25½: 27: 28: 28½: 28½: 30] in)

47 [50: 53: 56.5: 59: 61: 64.5: 67] cm
(18½ [19½: 21: 22: 23: 24: 25½: 26½] in)

Bute, from Rowan Magazine 52.

Looking at the photograph of this lovely cardigan, you may think that it is a fitted style, but if you look at the line drawing you can see that the body is in fact straight. The line drawing also shows you what type of sleeve head there is; a fitted sleeve in this instance.

The line drawing gives the main measurements, but as we go through the next couple of chapters, you will learn how to add a lot more detail to these drawings in order to get the fit you really need.

On the following pages you will find garments from Rowan collections and ideas as to how you could alter them to suit different body shapes. These will help you look at knitting patterns in a different way, and hopefully open you up to more garments you could make.

This cardigan is ideal for an apple-shaped body (see page 10), and also for an athletic shape (see page 12). It would work for a pear-shaped body (see page 11) and an hourglass figure (see page 13), but for those you may like to add some shaping.

SHAPED JACKET

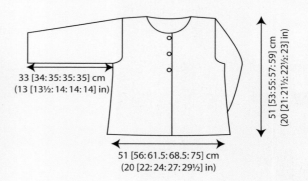

33 [34: 35: 35: 35] cm
(13 [13½: 14: 14: 14] in)

51 [53: 55: 57: 59] cm
(20 [21: 21½: 22½: 23] in)

51 [56: 61.5: 68.5: 75] cm
(20 [22: 24: 27: 29½] in)

Martha, from Rowan Magazine 55.

This cute little jacket is knitted in simple moss stitch. Looking at it in detail, the sleeves are three-quarter length, the body is shaped but fairly short, and the neck is quite wide. These are all areas that some of you may want to change (see pages 62–81). The sleeves are shallow set in.

This is a good jacket for a pear-shaped body (see page 11), as long as you make sure you have the length right, but an apple shape (see page 10) may want to avoid it.

BOXY JACKET

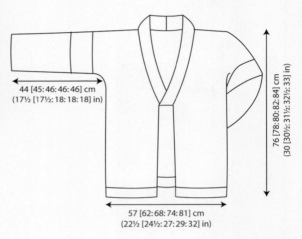

44 [45: 46: 46: 46] cm
(17½ [17½: 18: 18: 18] in)

76 [78: 80: 82: 84] cm
(30 [30½: 31½: 32½: 33] in)

57 [62: 68: 74: 81] cm
(22½ [24½: 27: 29: 32] in)

Boulevard, from Rowan brochure City Retreat.

This long-line, boxy jacket is great for many
shapes, but you may well prefer it to be
slightly more fitted (see pages 79–77) if you
are a pear shape (see page 11), and without
the dropped shoulders, especially if you
a larger lady (see page 17). With a fitted
shoulder (see page 70) it would be great for all
the apple shapes (see page 10) out there. The
sleeve shape is lovely, but with a wide cuff like
this it is imperative that the sleeve length is
correct (see page 68).

LONG-LINE JACKET

80 [82:84:86] cm
(31½ [32½: 33: 34] in)

45 [50: 56.5: 61.5] cm
(17½ [19½: 22: 24] in)

45 [46: 47: 47] cm
(17½ [18: 18½: 18½] in)

Harwood, from Rowan brochure Studio 2.

If you are a petite person who would like to look taller, the key to making this really lovely long-line jacket look good on you is to make sure the length measurement is exactly right (see page 66). It has two front pockets, so make sure that these sit in the right position for you; little worse than to go to put your hands in your pockets and they are down by your knees! The jacket is straight and relies on the stitch detail to give shape, but you could add more shaping if required (see pages 77–79). This is a great design for athletic shapes (see page 12).

SCOOP-NECK SWEATER

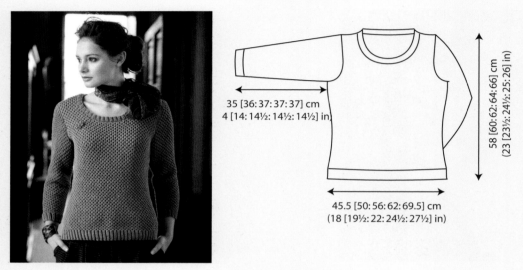

35 [36 : 37 : 37 : 37] cm
4 [14 : 14½ : 14½ : 14½] in

58 [60 : 62 : 64 : 66] cm
(23 [23½ : 24½ : 25 : 26] in)

45.5 [50 : 56 : 62 : 69.5] cm
(18 [19½ : 22 : 24½ : 27½] in)

Glenda, from Rowan Magazine 50.

A simple scoop-necked sweater – maybe too
wide a neck for some people (see page 80) –
with subtle shaping and fitted sleeves. The key
to this garment is getting the measurements
100 per cent correct. The really simple shape
would suit most bodies, but it is just perfect
for pear (see page 11) and hourglass
(see page 13) figures.

Short cardigan

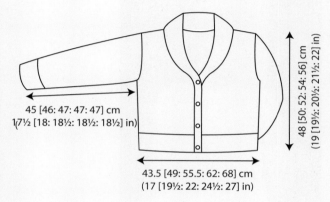

45 [46: 47: 47: 47] cm
1/7½ [18: 18½: 18½: 18½] in)

48 [50: 52: 54: 56] cm
(19 [19½: 20½: 21½: 22] in)

43.5 [49: 55.5: 62: 68] cm
(17 [19½: 22: 24½: 27] in)

Beatrix, from Rowan Magazine 52.

A short, boxy cardigan with very shallow
set-in sleeves. Not so many people can wear
something so short, but it would be easy to
lengthen the body (see page 66), and even add
shaping if needed (see pages 77–79). This
design will suit a pear-shaped body (see page
11) and also be good for a petite frame (see
page 15); make sure you measure the length
correctly and ensure that the shoulders fit well
(see page 74). This cardigan is also good for
an athletic shape (see page 12), but I would
layer it or make it a little longer.

ARAN SWEATER

33 [34: 35: 35: 35] cm
(13 [13½: 14: 14: 14] in)

47 [52.5: 58: 64: 70.5] cm
(18½ [20½: 23: 25: 28] in)

59 [61: 63: 65: 67] cm
(23 [24: 25: 25½: 26½] in)

Whiting, from Rowan brochure Wintertide.

This lovely sweater uses traditional Aran stitches with quite a modern shape: it is nice to see an Aran that is fitted because so often they are big and bulky. You may want to lengthen the sleeves (see page 68), and possibly make the body a little longer (see page 66): with such a deep rib, this style would suit pear shapes (see page 11). The neck may be too high, but it could easily be changed to a crew neck if needed (see page 80). If you were going with the shape as it is, the most important measurements would be shoulder width and sleeve circumference.

DROP-SLEEVE CARDIGAN

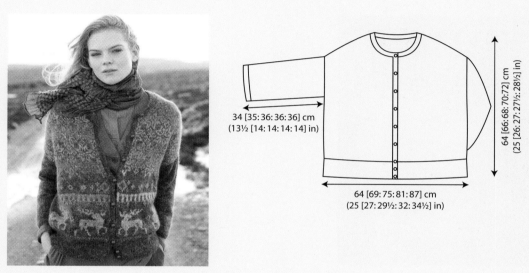

34 [35 : 36 : 36 : 36] cm
(13½ [14 : 14 : 14 : 14] in)

64 [66 : 68 : 70 : 72] cm
(25 [26 : 27 : 27½ : 28½] in)

64 [69 : 75 : 81 : 87] cm
(25 [27 : 29½ : 32 : 34½] in)

Wilhelmina, from Rowan brochure Nordic Tweed.

This is one of my favourites from this
collection. It is quite casual, and suitable for
lots of body shapes. I feel almost anybody
would feel good with this shape, though if
you are a plus size (see page 17) you may want
to make a more fitted sleeve (see page 70).

SHORT SWEATER

45 [46: 47: 47: 47] cm
(17½ [18: 18½: 18½: 18½] in)

48.5 [52.5: 59: 65.5: 71.5] cm
(19 [20½: 23: 26: 28] in)

(at centre back - front is 8cm shorter)
54 [56: 58: 60: 62] cm
(21 [22: 23: 23½: 24½] in)

Utsire, from Rowan Magazine 52.

This cute short sweater has a scooped
hemline that is lower in the back than in the
front. However, you can't tell that from the
photograph, so the line drawing is important
here. It is perfect for an athletic shape
(see page 12), though may need to be
lengthened for other shapes, something that is
easily done (see page 66).

ARAN TURTLE NECK SWEATER

43 [47: 51: 54: 54: 55: 55: 56] cm
[18½: 20: 21½: 21½: 21½: 21½: 22] in)

58 [61: 64: 67: 67: 69: 69: 72] cm
(23 [24: 25: 26½: 26½: 27: 27: 28½] in)

46.5 [50: 53.5: 56: 59: 61: 64: 66.5] cm
(18½ [19½: 21: 22: 23: 24: 25: 26] in)

Shannon, from Rowan Magazine 52.

This is a gorgeous Aran knit in Kid Classic
yarn. It has a high, slash neck that is quite
difficult to wear, so this may be the reason
some of you would decide not to make
this garment. But it is easy to give it a very
wearable crew neck (see page 80). I would
also check on the sleeve shaping and maybe
make it slightly more set-in (see page 70). The
overall shape is easy to wear and would suit
most body shapes, though it is especially good
for athletic (see page 12) and inverted triangle
(see page 14) figures.

Chapter 3

Taking body measurements

Now that you have an understanding of your body shape and some ideas as to the designs you could knit to flatter that shape, the next stage is the job of taking measurements to find out which size to make.

This can be done in two ways; by measuring your body and measuring garments that fit you, and I recommend a bit of both. Just measuring your body is not enough, as you need to add ease and also need to understand the fit of the garment. So as discussed in Chapter One (see page 19), hopefully you have put together a selection of garments from your wardrobe, with notes as to what you like and don't like about each one of them. Make sure you have a good selection of shapes and styles of garments: you will wear a casual sweater very differently to a fitted jacket.

When taking measurements from an existing garment, think about the fabric it is made from: is it a knitted fabric or a jersey knit that will stretch, or is a woven fabric that won't stretch? The garment you are going to knit will stretch a little bit, so bear that in mind. You may want to knit it a little smaller to allow for the stretch. Note that in the measurement instructions you sometimes need to add stitches for the seam allowance: I usually add two stitches for each individual seam allowance, for all styles of garment.

In this chapter you will find advice on the measurements you should take for various parts of your body and styles of garment. I have designed some basic body blocks for you to note all of your measurements on, and you'll find examples of them on the following pages, with blank versions on pages 87–94. These blocks offer the perfect way to record all of your measurement information for each type of garment you may wish to knit.

You will need a body block for each type of garment, as the fit you want will depend to a certain extent on where you'll wear it. For example, a loose-fitting, cosy, long-line cardigan to wear at home with leggings will require a different fit to a knitted jacket for going to work in, even if they are essentially a similar shape. So I suggest that you photocopy all the blank blocks and make your notes on the copies, keeping the versions in the book blank so that you can take new copies as needed: it is always good to go through this process with people that you knit for, too, so you have a record of all of their measurements.

You'll also find on page 45 an example of a record card, which is a helpful way of seeing all your measurements together: there's a blank version to photocopy on page 95. Again, I recommend photocopying one for every person whose measurements you want to note down.

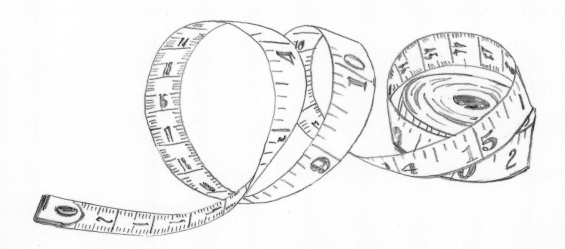

BASIC MEASUREMENTS: BODY BLOCK 1

Let's start with the simplest shape, a dropped-sleeve, straight sweater, and you will soon get the hang of taking measurements accurately.

Lay the garment completely flat, smoothing it out without overstretching it.

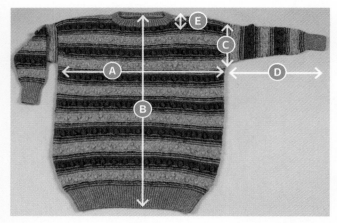

A *Width*
From side seam to side seam. Add seam allowance stitches: see page 34.

B *Length*
From back of neck, not including neckband, to lower edge.

C *Depth of armhole*
From shoulder to start of armhole shaping. It is important to measure in a straight line rather than on a curve.

D *Sleeve length*
From armhole down to cuff in a straight line, rather than following the sleeve seam.

E *Depth of neck*
From bottom of back neckband to top of front neck, below neckband.

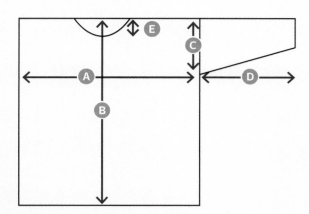

MEASUREMENTS FOR A FITTED SLEEVE: BODY BLOCK 2

Many straight garments have fitted sleeves/armholes. It is key to get the measurement across the shoulders correct so that the shoulders fit well and don't overhang. Make sure you are happy with the depth of armhole and circumference of the sleeve itself.

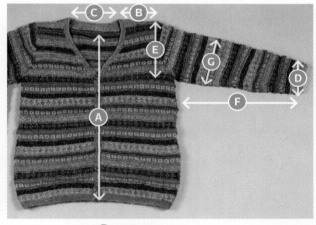

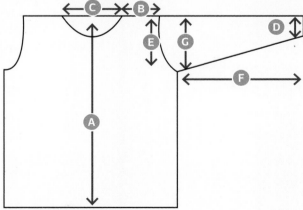

A *Length*
As Body Block 1 (see page 36).

B *Width of shoulder*
From sleeve head across to neck shaping, not including neckband.

C *Back neck*
Across back of neck, not including neckband.

D *Width of sleeve at cuff*
Width of the sleeve above cuff, then double that for full width. Add seam allowance stitches: see page 34.

E *Depth of armhole*
As Body Block 1 (see page 36).

F *Sleeve length*
As Body Block 1 (see page 36).

G *Width of sleeve at the top*
Width of the sleeve before sleeve top shaping, then double that for full width. Add seam allowance stitches: see page 34.

BUST AND HIP MEASUREMENTS: BODY BLOCK 3

If you have a garment that fits you well on the hips but is too baggy under the arms, then you will need to shape your knitted version differently. Put the garment on and ask a friend to pin it to fit under the arms so that you know what the width of your garment needs to be.

Don't worry that the shape doesn't match the line drawing of a standard pattern; this is about getting the fit to suit you.

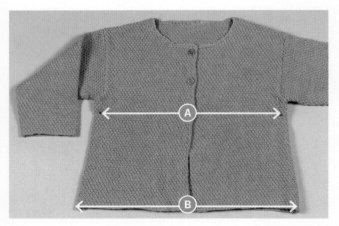

A *Width under the arms*
Width from pin to pin. Add seam allowance stitches: see page 34.

B *Width at hips*
From side seam to side seam at lower edge. Add seam allowance stitches: see page 34.

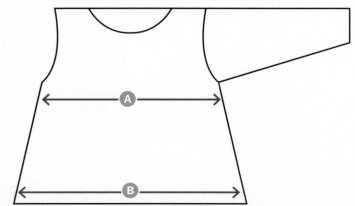

MEASUREMENTS FOR A FITTED GARMENT: BODY BLOCK 4

When making a shaped, fitted jacket or sweater it is imperative to take lots of measurements from a garment that fits you well, and then put them in to your chosen knitting pattern.

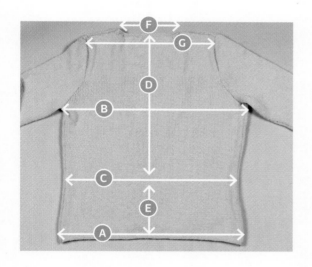

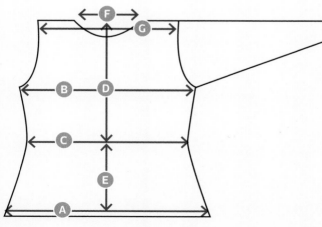

A *Width at hips*
As Body Block 3 (see page 38).

B *Width at bust*
From side seam to side seam at bust level. Add seam allowance stitches: see page 34.

C *Width at waist*
From side seam to side seam at waistline. Add seam allowance stitches: see page 34.

D *Length from back neck to waist*
From back neck, below neckband, down to waistline.

E *Length from waist to hem*
From waistline down to lower edge.

F *Back neck*
Across back of neck, not including neckband.

G *Width at shoulders*
From sleeve head across to other sleeve head.

MEASUREMENTS FOR A LONG-LINE GARMENT: BODY BLOCKS 5 AND 6

When measuring a cardigan or long-line jacket, think about the shaping, especially if it is fitted on the hips. Look to see where the side seams sits on you: it may be that you have a large bust or tummy and that the seam is stretched round towards the front. Or the garment might not meet in the front, but the back looks great. This means you may need a smaller back piece and larger front pieces, because if you just made a larger size then the back, too, would be larger and the whole garment far too big. There isn't anything wrong with having a smaller back piece than front pieces.

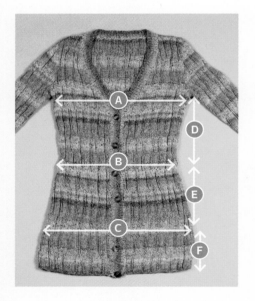

A *Width at bust*
From side seam to side seam at bust level. Add seam allowance stitches: see page 34.

B *Width at waist*
From side seam to side seam at waistline. Add seam allowance stitches: see page 34.

C *Width at hips*
From side seam to side seam at hip shaping. Add seam allowance stitches: see page 34.

D *Length waist to armhole*
From start of armhole shaping to waist shaping.

E *Length hip to waist*
From waist shaping to fullest part of hip shaping.

F *Length from hem to hip*
From hip shaping to lower edge.

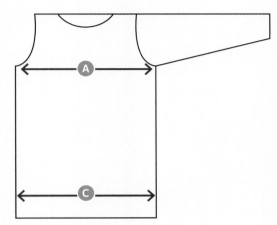

Loose-fitting long-line garment.

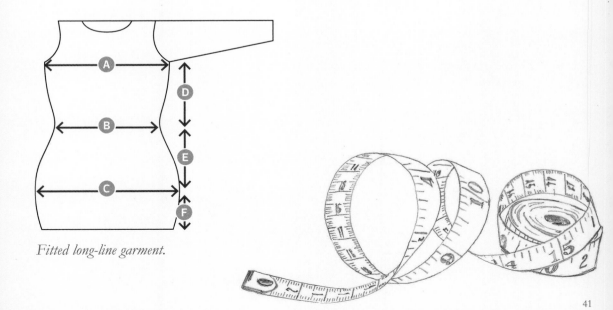

Fitted long-line garment.

MEASUREMENTS FOR A RAGLAN SLEEVE: BODY BLOCK 7

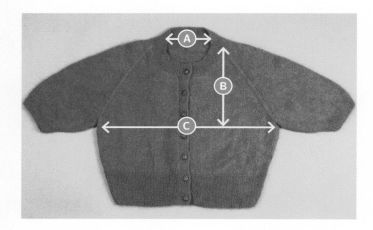

A flattering sleeve shape that is great for casual sweaters. A key measurement is the back neck; it is very easy to have too wide a neck with a raglan and then it doesn't sit very neatly.

A *Back neck*
Across back of neck, not including neckband.

B *Length of raglan*
From start of raglan shaping to top of raglan shaping in a straight line, not following raglan seam.

C *Width at bust*
From side seam to side seam at bust level. Add seam allowance stitches: see page 34.

MEASUREMENTS FOR A SHORT SWEATER: BODY BLOCK 8

For short, shaped sweaters that sit on the waist, the key thing to look at is the body length; remember that if you are going to have a snug, fitted welt then you need to allow some extra length for the sweater to pouch over the top. Also important for this garment to look great is the measurement for shoulders and back neck, to ensure the garment doesn't hang over your actual shoulders.

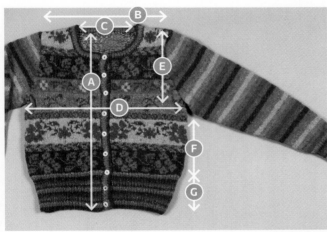

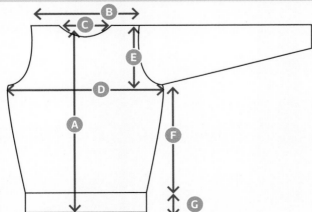

A *Length*
As Body Block 1 (see page 36).

B *Width at shoulders*
As Body Block 4 (see page 39).

C *Back neck*
As Body Block 1 (see page 36).

D *Width at bust*
As Body Block 7 (see page 42).

E *Depth of armhole*
As Body Block 2 (see page 37).

F *Length from armhole to top of welt*
From start of armhole shaping to top of welt in a straight line, not following curve of side seam.

G *Length of welt*
From top of welt to lower edge in a straight line, not following curve of welt.

Measurements from your body

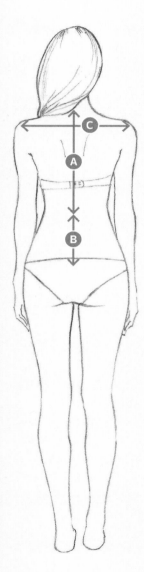

Maybe you don't have a perfectly fitting garment of the shape that you want to make. I still advise you to take basic measurements – such as width and length – from garments you do have, and then you can add in the rest by taking measurements from your body. You will need a friend to help you do this accurately: if you try to do it yourself, the results will certainly not be accurate because the bending and twisting you will need to do to get the tape measure in the right place will distort the result.

Key measurements to take from your body are:

A *Length to waist from nape of neck*
Measure down your back because it is flatter than your front.

B *Length from your waist to the hips*
To find out where your natural waist is, to put your hands on your waist and see where they sit comfortably. Or, tie a length of yarn around where you think your waist is: tie it snugly, but not tightly. Bend from side to side at the waist; the yarn will end up sitting on your natural waist.

C *Shoulders from top of arm*
With your arms relaxed down by your sides, measure straight across your back from the top of one arm to the top of the other.

PROJECT RECORD CARD

It is good practice to get into the habit of creating a record card for every project you knit, especially if you have made alterations to a design. On the card you can record all of the changes you made, which yarn you made it in; staple a ball band to the record card so you have details of the dye lot and washing instructions. You can also note the measurements you used and how many stitches or rows you have either added or taken away from which parts of the garment. This way, if you wish to recreate the project, all the design work is done.

Here is a sample card filled in: there is a blank one for you to photocopy on page 95.

PROJECT RECORD CARD

NAME OF PROJECT:
Bute cardigan

SOURCE OF PATTERN:
Rowan Magazine 52
page 14

YARN USED (NAME/BRAND/
COLOUR/FIBRE CONTENT):
Rowan Felted Tweed DK in Rage,
Ginger, Gilt and Camel

TENSION:
23 sts and 31 rows to 10cm

NEEDLE SIZE:
3.75mm

KEY MEASUREMENTS:
Length 43cm
Width of shoulders: 11cm
Back neck 14cm
Cuff width 12cm
Armhole depth 23cm
Sleeve length 25cm
Width of sleeve top 19cm

ALTERATIONS TO PATTERN:
Lengthened body by 2cm / 6 rows

Reduced width of body by 1cm / 3 stitches on
front and 2cm / 5 stitches on back.

Made each shoulder narrower by 1cm /
3 stitches, but kept back neck same width
as pattern.

Made left sleeve 2cm / 6 rows longer at
wrist, and right sleeve 1.5cm / 4 rows longer.

Chapter 4

Customising your body block

So, now that you have all the measurements needed, you need to utilise that information to create a body block that relates to the design you want to knit.

There will be a lot more measurements on your body block than on the line drawing that accompanies the pattern, but never fear, we are going to extract the pattern's measurements from the instructions so that you can see how they relate to your personal measurements.

We will work through a couple of examples – going from a straightforward drop-sleeve shoulder to a fully fitted garment – and then see what we need to do as far as alterations are concerned to ensure that the finished garment will fit you perfectly.

You will have to get the calculator out and do a bit of maths, but I am here to hold your hand, and once you have gone through the process a few times it will be easy. And it will open a whole new world of choosing what to knit! The pattern world will become your knitting oyster!

Let's get going…

TENSION

Before you start on the journey of creating the perfectly fitting sweater, you need to understand the importance of tension. We have all been in the position where we are so eager to cast on with the beautiful yarn we have just purchased that we ignore the tension and hope for the best. Well, that needs to change I'm afraid: it's time to get into tension!

The importance of tension is key in two different ways: the actual tension you achieve when knitting, and also, understanding what the tension quoted in the pattern means in order to extract the measurements you need to check that the garment will fit you.

THE TENSION YOU ACHIEVE WHEN KNITTING

Every Rowan pattern will tell you the tension the designer has used in order to calculate the number of stitches and rows. For example: '20 sts and 28 rows to 10cm measured over stocking stitch using 4mm needles'. You MUST knit a tension sample, before starting the oh-so-desirable project, to check that your tension matches that given.

Cast on at least four stitches more than the tension stated, so 24 stitches for the example above. This ensures the stitches you will measure will be whole stitches, and won't be sitting on the edge of the sample.

Work in the stitch pattern stated and for the number of rows stated, plus four rows more (so 32 rows in our example), for the same reasons as you cast on more stitches.

Cast off the sample and pin it out on an ironing board, without stretching the work. Place a pin two stitches in from the right-hand side. Take a tape measure and measure 10cm across from the pin, and place another pin. Now count the number of stitches between the two pins.

Then count the number of rows: place a pin, sideways, two rows down from the cast-off edge. Measure 10cm down from the pin, and place another pin. Count the rows between the pins.

The numbers of stitches and rows are your natural tension with that yarn and those needles, over that stitch pattern. But this will change depending on the yarn and stitch pattern you are using. So with a pure wool DK you might be spot on to a given pattern tension, but when working with a cotton DK yarn, your knitting may be a bit looser. So you need to knit a tension sample EVERY TIME you embark on a new project.

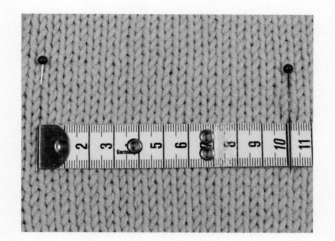

Measuring stitches in a tension square.

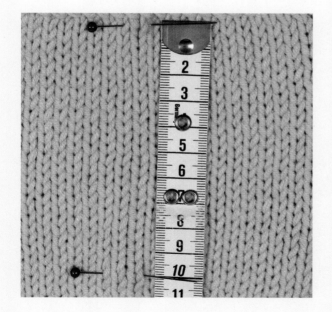

Measuring rows in a tension square.

CHANGING YOUR TENSION

First of all, every knitter has a 'natural' tension: when a new yarn comes into Rowan, several knitters are asked to work with it and the average of all their tensions is used to decide on a standard tension for that yarn. Sometimes the tension given in a pattern using a particular yarn is different to the standard tension given on the ball band for that yarn, and that is because the designer feels the fabric has to be tighter or looser for the particular design to work. So you need to ignore the standard tension and work to the designer's tension used in the pattern.

It may be that your tension is exactly the same as the pattern tension, which is fine and you can move forward. If it is out by one stitch, then changing your needle size can quickly rectify this.

For example, if your tension is 21 sts instead of 20 sts to 10cm, this means that your knitting is slightly tighter as you have fitted more stitches into the 10cm. If you use a knitting needle one size larger, you should gain the correct tension. Similarly, if you only have 19 sts in the 10cm, then your knitting is too loose and you would need to drop a needle size. If you are out by more than one stitch, you can try more sizes of knitting needles, or you may need to look at making the garment in a different size.

The impact of just one or two stitches can be considerable in a finished garment. Take, for example, a sweater that needs to be 60cm wide and the tension given is 20 sts to 10cm. If your tension is 22 sts to 10cm, this means you are 2 sts tighter every 10cm, so 12 sts tighter across 60cm. The original tension of 20 sts to 10cm breaks down as 2 sts to 1cm, so your garment will be 6cm too small on the back and 6cm too small on the front; 12cm too small all around! On average, this is a difference of two sizes.

The same principle applies if your stitches are too loose: the garment will be too big. At least you will fit into it, but it won't look nice and feel nice!

Don't ignore incorrect tension! And don't try to just knit a bit looser or tighter: your natural tension will quickly assert itself and all you'll end up with is uneven knitting, as well as a garment that doesn't fit!

It is also good to get into the habit of checking your measurements regularly throughout the project rather than waiting to cast off and then being disappointed, because some people's tension alters when they have more stitches on the needle.

EXTRACTING PATTERN INFORMATION USING THE TENSION COUNT

The other use of tension is to collect all the measurements you need in order to ensure that the fit of your garment will be correct and will suit you. The exercises set out on the following pages show you how to do this. Don't be put off by all the numbers, it is quite simple maths: have your calculator to hand.

Let us say that the tension quoted in a pattern is 29 sts and 38 rows to 10cm. The first thing to do is break that tension down to single units of 1cm.

Divide the 29 sts by 10 to give 2.9 sts to 1cm, and divide the 38 rows by 10 to give 3.8 rows to 1cm.

This allows you to calculate how wide a piece of knitting will be when you only have the number of stitches to go by. For example, if the piece is 145 sts wide, you simply divide 145 by 2.9 and you would then know the piece will be 50cm wide.

The same with the length: if is 60 rows, you divide 60 by 3.8 and you would then know the piece will measure 15.79cm.

EXTRACTING MEASUREMENTS FROM A PATTERN

Over the following pages we will work through three examples to show you how to extract the necessary information from a knitting pattern.

To keep it simple, I have started with the basics and then added in more complex measurements in subsequent examples. I suggest you look at each example rather than just go to the shape that you feel suits you.

If you can follow and understand how we have achieved these measurements, you can do anything! The theory is the same whatever shape you are trying to establish.

Each example lists the measurements you'll need, coded with a letter. On the relevant pattern the section required is highlighted and coded with the same letter.

Note that in all of the examples only the bits of the patterns needed are shown (so they are incomplete). Also, I have chosen to use the smallest size given, purely for simplicity. As different measurements are needed for different garments, the letter coding isn't consistent from one garment to the next.

PAIGE
LISA RICHARDSON
Main image page 78

YARN

	S	M	L	XL
To fit bust	81-86	91-97	102-107	112-117
	32-34	36-38	40-42	44-46

Kidsilk Haze

A Liqueur 595	4	4	5	5
B Marmalade 596	2	2	2	2
C Ember 644	4	4	5	6
D Jelly 597	4	4	5	5
E Fern 629	3	3	4	4

NEEDLES
1 pair 5mm (no 6) (US 8) needles
1 pair 6mm (no 4) (US 10) needles

TENSION
18 sts and 25 rows to 10 cm measured ove
using 6mm (US 10) needles and 3 strands o
yarn held together.

BACK
Using 5mm (US 8) needles and one strand
each of yarns A, B and C held together cast
on 92 [100: 112: 120: 136] sts.
Row 1 (RS): K3, *P2, K2, rep from * to
last st, K1.
Row 2: K1, P2, *K2, P2, rep from * to last st, K1.
These 2 rows form rib.
Work in rib for a further 4 rows, dec [inc: dec:
inc: dec] 1 st at end of last row and ending
with RS facing for next row.
91 [101: 111: 121: 135] sts.
Change to 6mm (US 10) needles.**
Beg with a K row, work in st st until back meas
17 cm, ending with RS facing for next row.
Cast on 3 sts at beg of next 2 rows.
97 [107: 117: 127: 141] sts.
***Place markers at both ends of last row.
Cont straight until back meas 8 [9: 9: 10: 10]
cm **from markers**, ending with RS facing
for next row.
Break off yarn B and join in yarn D.
Using one strand each of yarns A, C and D
held together, cont straight until back meas
23 [25: 25: 27: 27] cm **from markers**, ending
with RS facing for next row.
Break off yarn A and join in yarn E.

A

116

52

B

Using one strand each of yarns C, D and E held together, cont straight until back meas 34 [35: 36: 37: 38] cm **from markers**, ending with RS facing for next row.

C

D

Shape armholes
Cast off 5 sts at beg of next 2 rows.
87 [97: 107: 117: 131] sts.
Dec 1 st at each end of next and foll 3 alt rows.
79 [89: 99: 109: 123] sts.
Cont straight until work meas 38 [41: 41: 44: 44] cm **from markers**, ending with RS facing for next row.
Break off yarn C and join in yarn A.
Using one strand each of yarns A, D and E held together, complete work as folls:

E

Cont straight until armhole meas 21 [22: 23: 24: 25] cm, ending with RS facing for next row.
Shape shoulders and funnel neck
Cast off 7 [9: 10: 12: 14] sts at beg of next 4 rows, then 7 [8: 10: 11: 13] sts at beg of foll 2 rows. 37 [37: 39: 39: 41] sts.
Dec 1 st at each end of next and foll 2 alt rows. 31 [31: 33: 33: 35] sts.
Work a further 9 rows, ending with RS facing for next row.
Cast off **loosely**.

FRONT
Work as given for back to **.
Beg with a K row, work in st st until front meas ... cm, ending with RS facing for next row.
Cast on 3 sts at beg of next 2 rows. [107: 117: 127: 141] sts.
Complete as given for back from ***.

SLEEVES
5mm (US 8) needles and one strand of yarns A, B and C held together cast on ... 42: 42: 46] sts.
(RS): K2, *P2, K2, rep from * to end.
... P2, *K2, P2, rep from * to end.

These 2 rows form rib.
Work in rib for a further 4 rows, inc [dec: inc: inc: dec] 1 st at end of last row and ending with RS facing for next row.
39 [41: 43: 43: 45] sts.
Change to 6mm (US 10) needles.
Beg with a K row, work in st st, shaping sides by inc 1 st at each end of 3rd [3rd: 3rd: 3rd: next] and foll 0 [0: 0: 0: 1] alt row, then on 4 foll 4th rows. 49 [51: 53: 53: 57] sts.
Work 1 [1: 3: 3: 3] rows, ending with RS facing for next row.
Break off yarn B and join in yarn D.
Using one strand each of yarns A, C and D held together, cont in st st, inc 1 st at each end of 3rd [3rd: next: next: next] and 5 [5: 6: 6: 6] foll 4th rows. 61 [63: 67: 67: 71] sts.
Work 3 rows, ending with RS facing for next row.
Break off yarn A and join in yarn E.
Using one strand each of yarns C, D and E held together, cont in st st, inc 1 st at each end of next and 1 [2: 3: 6: 6] foll 4th rows, then on 3 [2: 2: 0: 0] foll 6th rows. 71 [73: 79: 81: 85] sts.
Work 3 [5: 3: 3: 3] rows, ending with RS facing for next row.
Break off yarn C and join in yarn A.
Using one strand each of yarns A, D and E held together, complete work as folls:
Inc 1 st at each end of 3rd [next: 3rd: next: 4th] and 1 [2: 1: 2: 2] foll 6th [6th: 6th: 4th: 4th] rows. 75 [79: 83: 87: 91] sts.
Cont straight until sleeve meas 40 [41: 42: 42: 42] cm, ending with RS facing for next row.
Shape top
Cast off 5 sts at beg of next 2 rows. 65 [69: 73: 77: 81] sts.
Dec 1 st at each end of next and foll 2 alt rows, then on foll row, ending with RS facing for next row.

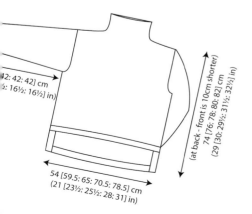

42: 42: 42] cm
½: 16½: 16½] in)

(at back - front is 10cm shorter)
74 [76: 78: 80: 82] cm
(29 [30: 29½: 31½: 32½] in)

54 [59.5: 65: 70.5: 78.5] cm
(21 [23½: 25½: 28: 31] in)

EXAMPLE 1
Paige, from Rowan Magazine 52.

For this simple drop-sleeve sweater I have
drawn a body block to match and marked with
arrows all the measurements I need to have in
order to check they suit my measurements.

*Note that the tension is 18 sts and 25 rows to
10cm. Broken down to single units, this is 1.8 sts
and 2.5 rows to 1cm.*

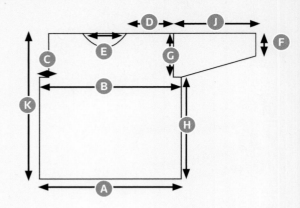

Ⓐ *Width at hem*
This measurement is shown on the pattern line
drawing, so no problem.

Ⓑ *Width at chest*
This is a straight garment, so it should have the
same number of stitches at the point before the
armhole shaping as at the cast on edge. Count
here is after shaping, so check back in pattern.

Ⓒ *Armhole shaping*
The number of stitches to be decreased for the
armhole, 9 stitches, divided by 1.8, gives 5cm.

Ⓓ *Shoulders*
Take the number of stitches for measurement
B, subtract the two lots of armhole decreases,
18 stitches, then subtract E (see below) and
divide by two (for two shoulders) , then by the
stitch unit. So, 97 - 18 - 31 = 48 ÷ 2 = 24 ÷ 1.8
= 13.33cm.

Ⓔ *Back of neck*
(This measurement is essential to know how
the neckline will sit on you: an average back

neck measurement is around 15cm for a
standard crew neck.) This calculation is shown
in Example 2 (see page 56), so I'll just tell you
that on this garment it is 31 sts. Divide this by
1.8 to give 17.2cm.

Ⓕ *Cuff*
The pattern says to cast on 38 sts, so divide 38
by 1.8 to give 21.1cm.

Ⓖ *Armhole depth*
The pattern says to knit until the armhole
measures 21cm.

Ⓗ *Length to armhole shaping*
The pattern says to knit until the work
measures 34cm.

Ⓙ *Sleeve length*
This measurement is shown on the pattern line
drawing, so no problem.

Ⓚ *Length from nape to hem*
This measurement is shown on the pattern line
drawing, so no problem.

PAIGE

LISA RICHARDSON

Main image page 78

YARN

	S	M	L	XL	XXL	
To fit bust						
	81-86	91-97	102-107	112-117	122-127 cm	
	32-34	36-38	40-42	44-46	48-50 in	

Kidsilk Haze

A	Liqueur 595					
	4	4	5	5	6	x 25gm
B	Marmalade 596					
	2	2	2	2	2	x 25gm
C	Ember 644					
	4	4	5	5	6	x 25gm
D	Jelly 597					
	4	4	4	5	5	x 25gm
E	Fern 629					
	3	3	3	4	4	x 25gm

NEEDLES

1 pair 5mm (no 6) (US 8) needles
1 pair 6mm (no 4) (US 10) needles

TENSION

18 sts and 25 rows to 10 cm measured over
using 6mm (US 10) needles and 3 strands of
yarn held together.

BACK

Using 5mm (US 8) needles and one strand
each of yarns A, B and C held together cast
on 92 [100: 112: 120: 136] sts.
Row 1 (RS): K3, *P2, K2, rep from * to
last st, K1.
Row 2: K1, P2, *K2, P2, rep from * to last st, K1.
These 2 rows form rib.
Work in rib for a further 4 rows, dec [inc: dec:
inc: dec] 1 st at end of last row and ending
with RS facing for next row.
91 [101: 111: 121: 135] sts.
Change to 6mm (US 10) needles.**
Beg with a K row, work in st st until back meas
17 cm, ending with RS facing for next row.
Cast on 3 sts at beg of next 2 rows.
97 [107: 117: 127: 141] sts.
***Place markers at both ends of last row.
Cont straight until back meas 8 [9: 9: 10: 10]
cm **from markers**, ending with RS facing
for next row.
Break off yarn B and join in yarn D.
Using one strand each of yarns A, C and D
held together, cont straight until back meas
23 [25: 25: 27: 27] cm **from markers**, ending
with RS facing for next row.
Break off yarn A and join in yarn E.

Using one strand each of yarns C, D and E
held together, cont straight until back meas
34 [35: 36: 37: 38] cm **from markers**, ending
with RS facing for next row.
Shape armholes
Cast off 5 sts at beg of next 2 rows.
87 [97: 107: 117: 131] sts.
Dec 1 st at each end of next and foll 3 alt rows.
79 [89: 99: 109: 123] sts.
Cont straight until work meas 38 [41: 41:
44: 44] cm **from markers**, ending with RS
facing for next row.
Break off yarn C and join in yarn A.
Using one strand each of yarns A, D and E held
together, complete work as foll:
Cont straight until back meas 21 [22: 23:
24: 25] cm, ending with RS facing for next
row.
Shape shoulders and funnel neck
Cast off 7 [9: 10: 12: 14] sts at beg of next
4 rows, then 7 [8: 10: 11: 13] sts at beg of foll
2 rows. 37 [37: 39: 39: 41] sts.
Dec 1 st at each end of next and foll 2 alt rows.
31 [31: 33: 33: 35] sts.
Work a further 9 rows, ending with RS facing
for next row.
Cast off **loosely**.

FRONT

Work as given for back to **.
Beg with a K row, work in st st until front meas
7 cm, ending with RS facing for next row.
Cast on 3 sts at beg of next 2 rows.
97 [107: 117: 127: 141] sts.
Complete as given for back from ***.

SLEEVES

Using 5mm (US 8) needles and one strand
each of yarns A, B and C held together cast on
38 [42: 42: 42: 46] sts.
Row 1 (RS): K2, *P2, K2, rep from * to end.
Row 2: P2, *K2, P2, rep from * to end.

These 2 rows form rib.
Work in rib for a further 4 rows, inc [dec: inc:
inc: dec] 1 st at end of last row and ending
with RS facing for next row.
39 [41: 43: 43: 45] sts.
Change to 6mm (US 10) needles.
Beg with a K row, work in st st, shaping sides
by inc 1 st at each end of 3rd [3rd: 3rd: 3rd:
next] and foll 0 [0: 0: 0: 1] alt row, then on
4 foll 4th rows. 49 [51: 53: 53: 57] sts.
Work 1 [1: 3: 3: 3] rows, ending with RS facing
for next row.
Break off yarn B and join in yarn D.
Using one strand each of yarns A, C and D
held together, cont in st st, inc 1 st at each end
of 3rd [3rd: next: next: next] and foll 5 [5: 6: 6: 6]
foll 4th rows. 61 [63: 67: 67: 71] sts.
Work 3 rows, ending with RS facing for
next row.
Break off yarn A and join in yarn E.
Using one strand each of yarns C, D and E
held together, cont in st st, inc 1 st at each end
of next and 1 [2: 3: 6: 6] foll 4th rows, then on
3 [2: 2: 0: 0] foll 6th rows.
71 [73: 79: 81: 85] sts.
Work 3 [5: 3: 3: 3] rows, ending with RS facing
for next row.
Break off yarn C and join in yarn A.
Using one strand each of yarns A, D and E
held together, complete work as foll:
Inc 1 st at each end of 3rd [next: 3rd: next:
next] and 1 [2: 1: 2: 2] foll 6th [6th: 6th: 4th:
4th] rows. 75 [79: 83: 87: 91] sts.
Cont straight until sleeve meas 40 [41: 42:
42: 42] cm, ending with RS facing for
next row.
Shape top
Cast off 5 sts at beg of next 2 rows.
65 [69: 73: 77: 81] sts.
Dec 1 st at each end of next and foll 2 alt rows,
then on foll row, ending with RS facing for
next row.

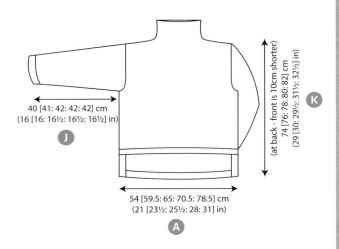

40 [41: 42: 42: 42] cm
(16 [16: 16½: 16½: 16½] in)

54 [59.5: 65: 70.5: 78.5] cm
(21 [23½: 25½: 28: 31] in)

(at back - front is 10cm shorter)
74 [76: 78: 80: 82] cm
(29 [30: 29½: 31½: 32½] in)

EXAMPLE 2
Bute, from Rowan Magazine 52.

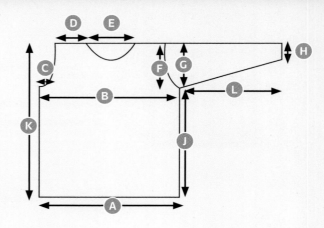

This is a simple cardigan with armhole shaping. Measurement D, the shoulder width, is key to this looking good.

Note that the tension is 25 sts and 30 rows to 10cm. Broken down to single units, this is 2.5 sts and 3 rows to 1cm.

A *Width at hem*
This measurement is shown on the pattern line drawing, so no problem.

B *Width at chest*
This is a straight garment, so it should have the same number of stitches at the cast on edge as at the point before the armhole shaping.

C *Armhole shaping*
For the armholes, there are 117 sts in the Back before shaping and 87 sts afterwards, so 30 sts in total were decreased, 15 sts on each armhole. Divide 15 by 2.5 to give 6cm.

D *Shoulders*
You can use the 87 sts from when all the decreases for armholes are complete, then subtract the back neck measurement E (see below) and divide by two (for two shoulders), then by the stitch unit. So, 87 − 37 = 50 ÷ 2 = 25 ÷ 2.5 = 10cm.

E *Back of neck*
The pattern says to cast off the centre 37 sts, so divide 37 by 2.5 to give 14.8cm.

F *Armhole depth*
The pattern says to knit until the armhole measures 18cm.

G *Sleeve width at top*
The pattern says to work increases until 89 sts, so divide 89 by 2.5 to give 35.6cm.

H *Cuff*
The pattern says 55 sts after the increases at the top of the cuff, so divide 55 by 2.5 to give 22cm.

J *Length to armhole shaping*
The pattern says to knit until the work measures 43cm.

K *Length from nape to hem*
This measurement is shown on the pattern line drawing, so no problem.

L *Sleeve length*
This measurement is shown on the pattern line drawing, so no problem.

BUTE
LISA RICHARDSON

Main image page 10 & 11

YARN

	XXS	XS	S	M	L	XL	XXL	2XL		
To fit bust/chest										
	91	97	102	107	112	117	122	127	cm	
	36	38	40	42	44	46	48	50	in	

Felted Tweed and Colourspun

1st colourway

A FTw Camel 157										
	2	2	2	3	3	3	3	3	x 50gm	
B Csp Pen-Y-Ghent 271										
	2	2	2	3	3	3	3	3	x 50gm	
C FTw Avocado 161										
	1	1	1	1	1	2	2	2	x 50gm	
D FTw Pine 158										
	1	1	1	2	2	2	2	2	x 50gm	
E FTw Phantom 153										
	2	2	2	2	2	2	2	3	x 50gm	
F Csp Buttertubs 270										
	3	3	3	3	4	4	4	4	x 50gm	
G FTw Paisley 171										
	1	1	1	2	2	2	2	2	x 50gm	

SPECIAL NOTE

This is a unisex design. To see the mens version please go to www.knitrowan.com to see the Rowan digital magazine 52.

NEEDLES

1 pair 3¼mm (no 10) (US 3) needles
1 pair 4mm (no 8) (US 6) needles
3¼mm (no 10) (US 3) circular needle,
120 cm long

BUTTONS - 7 x 137CC from Coats Crafts. Please see information page for contact details.

EXTRAS - Pair of purchased suede elbow patches

TENSION

25 sts and 30 rows to 10 cm measured over patt using 4mm (US 6) needles.

BACK

Using 3¼mm (US 3) needles and yarn F cast on 103 [111: 117: 125: 131: 135: 143: 147] sts.
Work in g st for 7 rows, ending with **WS** facing for next row.
Row 8 (WS): K6 [3: 6: 2: 5: 8: 3: 7], M1, (K7 [8: 7: 8: 8: 7: 8: 7], M1) 13 [13: 15: 15: 15: 17: 17: 19] times, K6 [4: 6: 3: 6: 8: 4: 7].
117 [125: 133: 141: 147: 153: 161: 167] sts.
Change to 4mm (US 6) needles.
Beg and ending rows as indicated and repeating

the 4 st patt rep 28 [30: 32: 34: 36: 38: 40: 41] times across each row, using the **fairisle** technique as described on the information page and repeating the 44 row patt repeat throughout, cont in patt from chart for back, which is worked in a combination of st st and rev st st beg with a K row, as follows:
Cont in patt until back meas 43 [44: 45: 46: 44: 44: 44: 46] cm, ending with RS facing for next row.

Shape armholes
Keeping patt correct, cast off 5 sts at beg of next 2 rows.
107 [115: 123: 131: 137: 143: 151: 157] sts.
Dec 1 st at each end of next 5 rows, then on foll 4 alt rows, then on foll 4th row.
87 [95: 103: 111: 117: 123: 131: 137] sts.
Cont straight until armhole meas 18 [20: 22: 24: 26: 28: 28: 29] cm, ending with RS facing for next row.

Shape shoulders and back neck
Next row (RS): Cast off 7 [9: 10: 11: 12: 13: 14: 15] sts, patt until there are 18 [20: 22: 25: 26: 28: 30: 32] sts on right needle and turn, leaving rem sts on a holder.
Work each side of neck separately.
Dec 1 st at neck edge of next 3 rows, ending with RS facing for next row, **and at same time** cast off 7 [9: 10: 11: 12: 13: 14: 15] sts at beg of 2nd row.
Cast off rem 8 [8: 9: 11: 11: 12: 13: 14] sts.
With RS facing, rejoin yarns to rem sts, cast off centre 37 [37: 39: 39: 41: 41: 43: 43] sts, patt to end.
Complete to match first side, reversing shapings.

SLEEVES

Using 3¼mm (US 3) needles and yarn F cast on 49 [51: 55: 57: 59: 59: 63: 65] sts.
Work in g st for 7 rows, ending with **WS** facing for next row.
Row 8 (WS): K4 [3: 5: 3: 4: 5: 3: 4], M1, (K8 [9: 9: 10: 10: 7: 8: 8], M1) 5 [5: 5: 5: 5: 7: 7: 7] times, K5 [3: 5: 4: 5: 5: 4: 5].
55 [57: 61: 63: 65: 67: 71: 73] sts.
Change to 4mm (US 6) needles.
Beg and ending rows as indicated and repeating the 4 st patt rep 13 [14: 15: 15: 16: 16: 17: 18]

times across each row, using the **fairisle** technique as described on the information page and repeating the 44 row patt repeat throughout, cont in patt from chart for sleeve, which is worked in a combination of st st and rev st st beg with a K row, as follows:
Inc 1 st at each end of 5th and every foll 6th row to 83 [81: 73: 73: 83: 91: 79: 77] sts, then on every foll 8th row until there are 89 [93: 97: 101: 105: 109: 109: 111] sts, taking inc sts into patt.
Cont straight until sleeve meas 43 [47: 51: 54: 54: 55: 55: 56] cm, ending with RS facing for next row.

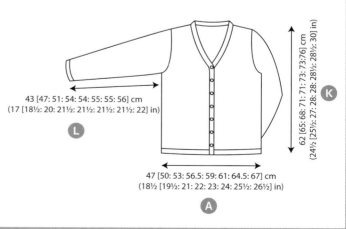

43 [47: 51: 54: 54: 55: 55: 56] cm
(17 [18½: 20: 21½: 21½: 21½: 21½: 22] in)

62 [65: 68: 71: 71: 73: 73:76] cm
(24½ [25½: 27: 28: 28: 28½: 28½: 30] in)

47 [50: 53: 56.5: 59: 61: 64.5: 67] cm
(18½ [19½: 21: 22: 23: 24: 25½: 26½] in)

EXAMPLE 3
Kintyre, from Rowan Magazine 52.

With this fully shaped sweater we will
concentrate on the measurements that
affect the shaping and the length of
shaping; because we all have differing
body lengths, these are key when making a
fully fitted piece. You still need the other
important measurements; just refer to
the other examples shown previously to
see how to extract that information.

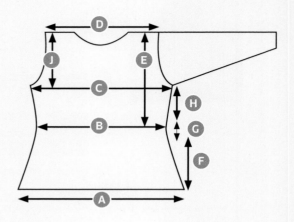

*Note that the tension is 27 sts and 27 rows to 10cm. Broken down to single units,
this is 2.7 sts and 2.7 rows to 1cm.*

Ⓐ *Width at hem*
This measurement is shown on the pattern
line drawing, so no problem.

Ⓑ *Width at waist*
The pattern says you should have 103 sts after
the decreases, so divide 103 by 2.7 to give
38.14cm.

Ⓒ *Width at chest*
The pattern says you should have 113 sts after
the increases, so divide 113 by 2.7 to give
41.85cm. Note: this is the same measurement
as measurement A, but this isn't always the
case. And people rarely have identical bust
and hip measurements, so make sure you look
at what you need.

Ⓓ *Width at shoulders*
The pattern says you should have 87 sts after
the armhole decreases, so divide 87 by 2.7 to
give 32cm.

Ⓔ *Length from neck to waist*
A key length measurement for which you need
J + H + half of G (to arrive at the actual
waistline), so 18 + 17.96 + 3.15 = 39.11cm.

Ⓕ *Length from hem to waist*
You need to add up all of the rows, including
those giving you the decrease instructions,
which comes to 29 rows, so divide 29 by 2.7
to give 10.74cm

Ⓖ *Length of waist shaping*
The pattern says to work 17 rows straight, so
divide 17 by 2.7 to give 6.3cm.

H Length from waist to armhole shaping

The pattern says that the work should measure 35cm from the lower edge, so subtract measurements G and F: 35 – 6.3 – 10.74 = 17.96cm.

J Armhole height

The pattern says to knit until the armhole measures 18cm.

KINTYRE
MARIE WALLIN
Main image page 14 & 15

● ● ●

SIZES

	S	M	L	XL	XXL
To fit bust					
	81-86	91-97	102-107	112-117	122-127 cm
	32-34	36-38	40-42	44-46	48-50 in

YARN

Wool Cotton, Kidsilk Haze and Pure Wool DK

A WCo Mocha 965						
	2	3	3	3	4	x 50gm
B *KSH Blackcurrant 641						
	1	1	1	2	2	x 25gm
C WCo Deepest Olive 907						
	2	2	2	3	3	x 50gm
D *KSH Fudge 658						
	2	2	2	2	3	x 25gm
E WCo Ship Shape 955						
	1	1	1	1	1	x 50gm
F PWDK Ox Blood 049						
	2	2	2	2	2	x 50gm
G *KSH Brick 649						
	1	1	1	1	1	x 25gm
H *KSH Liqueur 595						
	1	1	1	1	1	x 25gm
I WCo Coffee Rich 956						
	4	5	5	6	6	x 50gm
J WCo Windbreak 984						
			1	1	1	x 50gm

*Kidsilk Haze is used DOUBLE throughout

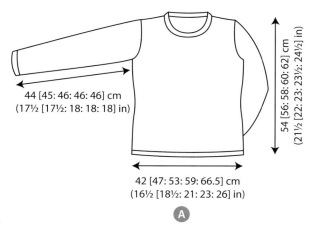

44 [45: 46: 46: 46] cm
(17½ [17½: 18: 18: 18] in)

42 [47: 53: 59: 66.5] cm
(16½ [18½: 21: 23: 26] in)

54 [56: 58: 60: 62] cm
(21½ [22: 23: 23½: 24½] in)

NEEDLES
1 pair 3¼mm (no 10) (US 3) needles

TENSION
27 sts and 27 rows to 10 cm measured over patterned st st using 3¼mm (US 3) needles.

BACK
Using 3¼mm (US 3) needles and yarn E cast on 113 [127: 143: 159: 179] sts.
Row 1 (RS): K1, *P1, K1, rep from * to end.
Row 2: As row 1.
These 2 rows form moss st.
Work in moss st for a further 2 rows, ending with RS facing for next row.
Beg and ending rows as indicated and using the **fairisle** technique as described on the information page, cont in patt from chart for body, which is worked entirely in st st beg with a K row, as folls:
Work 4 [4: 6: 6: 8] rows, ending with RS facing for next row.
Keeping patt correct, dec 1 st at each end of next and 2 foll 6th rows, then on 2 foll 4th rows. 103 [117: 133: 149: 169] sts.
Work 17 rows, ending with RS facing for next row.
Inc 1 st at each end of next and 4 foll 8th rows, taking inc sts into patt.
113 [127: 143: 159: 179] sts.
Cont straight until chart row 90 [94: 96: 98: 102] has been completed, ending with RS facing for next row. (Back should meas approx 35 [36: 37: 38: 39] cm.)
Shape armholes
Keeping patt correct, cast off 5 [6: 7: 8: 9] sts at beg of next 2 rows. 103 [115: 129: 143: 161] sts.
Dec 1 st at each end of next 5 [7: 7: 9: 13] rows, then on foll 3 [5: 8: 8: 9] alt rows.
87 [91: 99: 109: 117] sts.
Cont straight until chart row 138 [146: 150: 154: 162] has been completed, ending with RS facing for next row. (Armhole should meas approx 18 [19: 20: 21: 22] cm.)
Shape shoulders and back neck
Next row (RS): Cast off 7 [7: 8: 10: 11] sts,

USING YOUR CUSTOMISED PATTERN BODY BLOCK

You now know what your ideal measurements are (see Chapter 3), and you can now use the principles given on pages 54–59 to extract from a pattern the corresponding measurements of the garment you would like to make. Write all these measurements down on personal pattern body blocks (use one of those given on pages 87–94). Then put the two sets of measurements side-by-side and see what you can establish.

First of all, highlight the areas where the measurements match. This may be very straightforward; if they match one of the sizes you can get straight on with knitting it. Or it may be the case that the width and body length match, but when it comes to length of sleeve or width of back neck they are different, so this is where you can make some simple changes in order to change the garment from okay to fantastic!

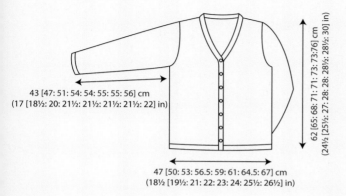

43 [47: 51: 54: 54: 55: 55: 56] cm
(17 [18½: 20: 21½: 21½: 21½: 21½: 22] in)

62 [65: 68: 71: 71: 73: 73:76] cm
(24½ [25½: 27: 28: 28: 28½: 28½: 30] in)

47 [50: 53: 56.5: 59: 61: 64.5: 67] cm
(18½ [19½: 21: 22: 23: 24: 25½: 26½] in)

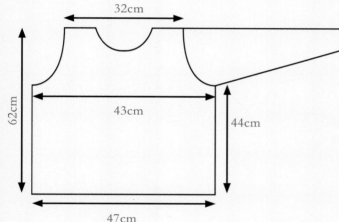

32cm

43cm

44cm

62cm

47cm

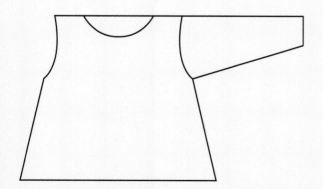

Looking at this example, you can see that the smallest pattern size is on the whole a good fit, but the person's smaller bust measurement means that where the pattern asks you to knit straight up the side, you in fact need to decrease for the smaller bust. The lady this body block belongs to has probably always knitted the straight cardigan and had all of this bulk under her arms and bust and just assumed that that was the way it had to be.

The shoulder measurement is shorter, too, so more decreasing needs to happen at the armholes in order to get a good fit on the shoulders. If you have narrow shoulders there is nothing worse than having the shoulder seams hanging down the tops of your arms and making you look bigger than you are.

The actual shape this lady needs is more like that shown left.

CHAPTER 5
CUSTOMISING A KNITTING PATTERN

So here we are in Chapter 5: we have looked at our shape, measured our favourite garments and our bodies, found some designs that we would like to make, and compared the measurements to our own body block. So now the interesting part starts.

First of all don't panic, I am going to be with you every step of the way. I have broken this chapter down step-by-step to show you how to alter the width for a straight garment and a shaped garment, then the length, moving onto a sleeve, and so on. Follow the directions carefully and methodically and it will all fall into place.

I have kept to standard garment shapes, but all the skills are covered for altering all shapes and sizes: if you work though this chapter in full you will soon learn how you can apply the calculations to whatever you wish to alter or design.

For convenience I have used a tension of 20 sts and 28 rows to 10cm throughout, unless otherwise stated.

Let's get started…

When looking at altering the width of a sweater or cardigan you have to think about a couple of things:

Is the garment straight up to the armholes?

Is it heavily patterned with either colour or texture?

Let's do a plain garment first to become familiar with the process, then we will discuss patterned garments.

This line drawing shows a garment that is straight up to the armholes, and in this example we would like to increase the width by 5cm – although the same theory applies when decreasing the width.

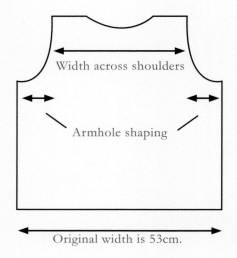

Width across shoulders

Armhole shaping

Original width is 53cm.

1. Calculate the tension over 1cm: in this instance 2 sts and 2.8 rows.

2. Calculate how many stitches wide the original garment is: 53cm x 2 sts = 106 sts. (You would also find this information in the pattern, but always worth a double check.)

3. Calculate how many stitches you need to add: 5cm x 2 sts = 10 sts.

4. So you need to cast on 116 sts in order to get the width required.

Now, if this was a straight, dropped-sleeve garment you would work all the way to the top and put 5 sts either side of the neck for each shoulder. Then you would have to think about the sleeves; as you've added to the shoulders you will most probably need to reduce the length of the sleeves (see page 68).

However, if the garment has an armhole, as on the diagram here, you will need to think a little bit more. Quite often we need extra width around our tummy or bust, but not on our shoulders, and if you just kept the extra stitches all the way up to the shoulders you may find the sleeve seams are down your arms rather than sitting nicely on your shoulders.

Check the measurement across your shoulders (see page 44) and then calculate the sizes of the shoulders and armholes in the pattern (pages 56–57). If the extra stitches are not needed at the shoulders, you will need to add extra decreases in the armholes to achieve the required shoulder width.

If the garment is shaped and you require the extra width throughout the garment, then work the extra 10 stitches (or however many you require) throughout, remembering that it is +10 when the pattern gives the number of stitches you should have after a set of increases or decreases. If you don't want the extra width throughout, then turn to Altering The Shape Of A Body Piece (see page 75).

When altering the width of a patterned garment you need to think about how you will insert the extra stitches into the pattern. If it is a Fair Isle then usually you can add in a repeat. For an intarsia piece you may need to add in stitches at the side, or sometimes disperse the stitches across the row and mark them onto the chart to keep track of them.

Lace is the trickiest: it's always best to knit a sample piece and understand the pattern repeat. You may be restricted as to how many stitches you can add; for example, if you need 10 extra stitches but the lace has an 8-stitch repeat, then you would have to go with 8 or 16 stitches.

When working with Aran patterns, there is usually a panel of flat stitches, such as moss stitch or reverse stocking stitch, at the edge of a piece. It's tempting, but adding a lot of stitches here may not look so good: it will usually look best to to add them evenly between the cables.

ALTERING BODY LENGTH

As with altering width (see page 64), when looking at altering the length of a garment you have to think about a couple of things:

Is the garment straight up to the armholes?

Is it heavily patterned with either colour or texture?

When working on a plain, straight garment, as shown in the line drawing here, the sides are straight up until the armholes, and in this example we would like to increase the length by 8cm.

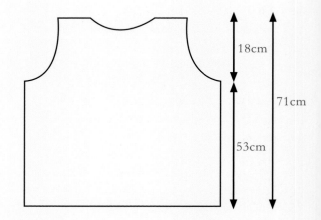

1 First of all establish the armhole depth by reading the pattern; it will tell you how long to work the armhole. Then take this away from the overall length of the garment to give you a measurement from the hem to the armhole. (This measurement may well be given in the pattern, but this exercise is to show you how you can calculate it yourself.)

2 Calculate the tension over 1cm: in this instance 2 sts and 2.8 rows.

3 Calculate how many rows long the original garment is: 53cm x 2.8 rows = 148 rows. (always round up or down to whole numbers or rows or stitches).

4 Calculate how many rows you need to add: 8cm x 2.8 rows = 22 rows.

5 So you need to knit 170 rows in order to get the length required.

If your garment is in plain stocking stitch you don't need to make this calculation; you can simply add (or subtract) the extra centimetres into the knitting before the armhole. However, you do need to know the exact number of rows if you are making a patterned garment that is shown on a chart.

You don't have to add or take away the rows all in one go, you could disperse them throughout the work evenly.

When you want to alter the length of a shaped garment, there are a few more things to think about (see page 77).

When looking at altering the sleeve width it makes a difference if the garment is in plain stocking stitch or is heavily patterned.

Here, we are working on a plain stocking stitch sleeve, shaped as shown in the line drawing, and need to know how many stitches to add or loose.

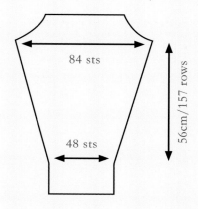

1 Calculate the tension over 1cm: in this instance 2 sts and 2.8 rows.

2 Calculate how many extra stitches you need for the sleeve. It may be that the lower sleeve is okay, but you need extra width at the top of the arm. Here, we would like to add an extra 3cm around the top of the arm

3 Calculate how many extra stitches are needed: 2 sts x 3cm = 6 sts extra. So the sleeve will increase from 48 stitches at the cuff to 84 stitches just below the sleeve head shaping.

4 Look at the pattern and establish how many stitches you have at the top of the cuff (48 in this instance), and then how many you have after all the increases (78 in this instance).

5 Calculate how many increases you need to do by subtracting the starting number of stitches (48) from the final number of stitches (84), so here 36 stitches need to be increased. You increase on both sides, so 18 increases need to be achieved in the sleeve length of 157 rows.

6 Divide the 157 rows by the amount of increases 157 ÷18 = 8.7. This means that if you increase on every eighth row you would achieve the amount of stitches needed at row 144 (18 x 8 = 144). You can't increase every ninth row as you'd have to cast off before making the last increase (18 x 9 = 162). But you can work the increases at different rates to fit them all in neatly (see page 69).

Altering the sleeve width will have an effect on the sleeve head shaping (see page 70).

As with altering the sleeve width (see page 67), here we are working on a plain sleeve, shaped as shown in the line drawing. We would like to reduce the length by 3cm.

1 Calculate the tension over 1cm: in this instance 2 sts and 2.8 rows.

2 Calculate how many rows are needed to achieve the new length: 53cm x 2.8 rows = 148 rows. (always round up or down to whole numbers or rows or stitches).

3 Look at the pattern and establish how many stitches you have at the top of the cuff (48 in this instance), and then how many you have after all the increases (78 in this instance).

4 Calculate how many increases you need to do by subtracting the starting number of stitches (48) from the final number of stitches (78), so here 30 stitches need to be increased. You increase on both sides, so 15 increases need to be achieved in the 148 rows.

5 Now divide the 148 rows by the amount of increases 148 ÷ 15 = 9.86. This means that if you increase on every ninth row you would achieve the number of stitches required at row 135, which is a bit early, but if you increase on every tenth row you wouldn't achieve the correct amount of stitches before having to cast off. But you can work the increases at different rates to fit them all in neatly (see opposite).

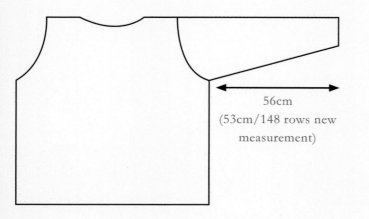

56cm
(53cm/148 rows new measurement)

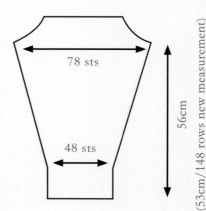

78 sts

48 sts

56cm

(53cm/148 rows new measurement)

Your choices are either to draw this out on graph paper, as shown below, or calculate the numbers. As you know if you have done any knitting, it is easier to increase on an even-numbered row. So for this example you could increase on every eighth or tenth row.

It's best to work the most frequent increases first then the less frequent, so you could do five sets of increases on every 8th row and then 10 sets of increases on every every tenth row. This will take you to row 140, so you then have just 8 rows straight before the sleeve head shaping, which stays unaltered.

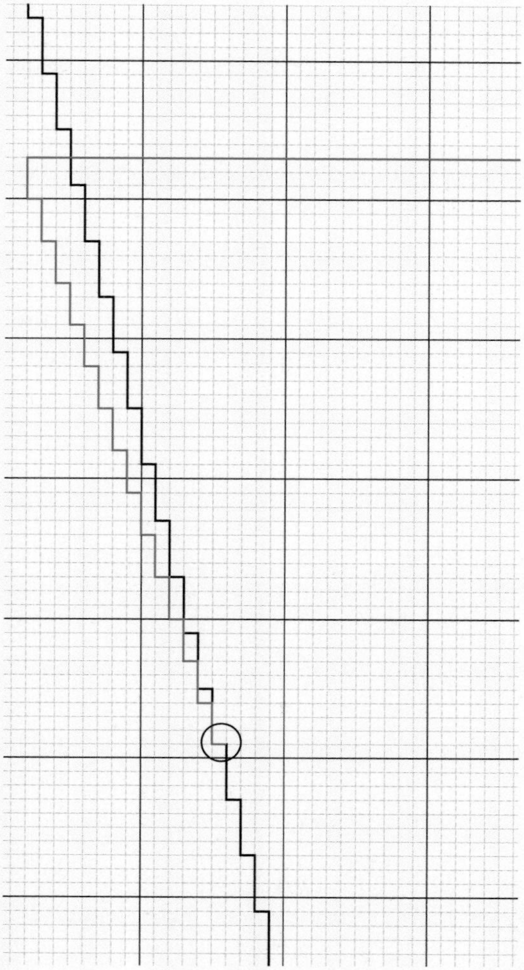

The black line shows the original pattern increases, and the green line shows the alteration.

The usual reason for altering a sleeve head is because you have altered the number of stitches in the sleeve, and this usually goes hand-in-hand with altering the depth of the armhole. (If you are a plus-size person the armhole is a key place to look at altering.) So, you are usually increasing the width of the top of the sleeve by the same measurement that you are altering the depth of the armhole. If not, then you should be!

Therefore, if you are increasing the armhole depth by 3cm and increasing the sleeve width at the top of the sleeve by 6cm, you would simply work the sleeve head exactly as the pattern instructions, but remembering that whenever they give you a stitch count you add the extra stitches on. For example, if you have added 10 stitches to the sleeve, then when all the decreases are complete before the sleeve head shaping and the pattern says you should have 35 stitches, you will have 45 stitches.

Another reason for altering the sleeve head will be if you are introducing an armhole into a garment that has been designed as a drop-sleeve. This is when you will need to calculate how to shape your sleeve head,

If it is a shallow, set-in sleeve (as shown in the design on page 25), you will work the armhole shaping for the front exactly the same as for the back, work one extra row then cast off.

If you want a fully fitted sleeve, then you will need to follow this procedure.

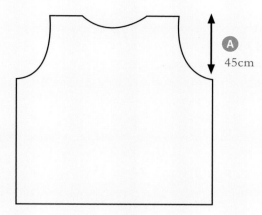

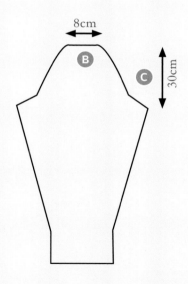

A When you reach the armhole shaping part of the garment front, work the armhole shaping exactly the same as for the back of the design.

B You always have a plateau at the top of a sleeve head (to fit onto the shoulder seam) that usually measures around 8cm (measurement B), which in terms of stitches is 8cm x 2 sts = 16 sts.

C Calculate how deep the sleeve head needs to be (measurement C). This is usually two-thirds of the armhole depth (measurement A). For example, if the armhole depth is 45cm, two-thirds of this will be 30cm. Then work this out as a number of rows: 30 x 2.8 = 84 rows.

The next step is to plot all of this onto graph paper. Turn to pages 72–73 to see how to do this.

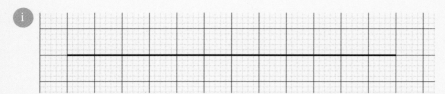

i. Draw a horizontal line the width of the number of stitches at the top of the sleeve increases

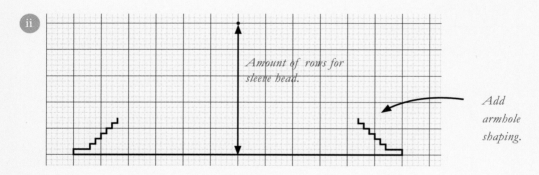

Amount of rows for sleeve head.

Add armhole shaping.

ii. Draw in the decreases for the armhole shaping. Count the amount of rows for the sleeve head from the beginning of the chart up to the centre point.

Calculate sleeve top.

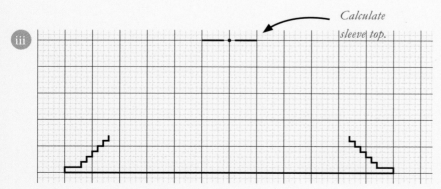

iii. Mark the centre plateau stitches.

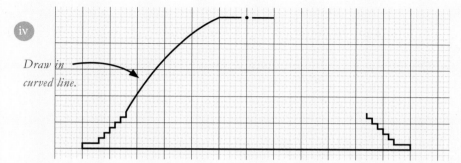

Draw in curved line.

iv. Then, on one side, draw in a curved line between the armhole shaping and the centre plateau.

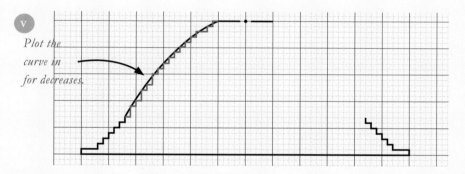

Plot the curve in for decreases.

v. Plot the decreases you need to make, following the curve. Duplicate them on the other side to make a symmetrical sleeve head.

It may be that you have altered the width of a garment, or it may be that the width of the torso part of a garment is fine but you have narrow shoulders and so need to alter the width of the shoulder measurement. As discussed in chapter 1, this measurement is key to making your garment look good when you are wearing it; nothing looks worse than a garment that falls off of your shoulders. Turn to page 44 to understand how to measure the required shoulder width correctly.

1 Calculate the tension over 1cm: in this instance 2 sts and 2.8 rows.

2 The measurements shown in this example have the width of the body before armhole shaping at 47cm and the shoulder width at 35cm. Taking one away from the other it tells us the armhole decreases add up to 6cm each.

3 If, for example, we need to reduce the shoulder width to 31cm, take 31cm from the body width of 47cm to give 16cm for the two armhole shapings, so 8cm each instead of 6cm. To work out how many stitches the extra 2cm equals, multiply that measurement by 2 stitches to know that you need to decrease 4 stitches more per armhole. So when working the armhole decreases you would work four more decreases than

the pattern states in order to bring the shoulder measurement down to 31cm.

4 Then, when you reach the back neck and shoulder shaping, you keep the back neck number of stitches the same and have 4 stitches less for each shoulder. Divide those 4 stitches evenly across the shoulder shaping.

5 To increase the shoulder width, you work in the same way, but adding rather than subtracting stitches.

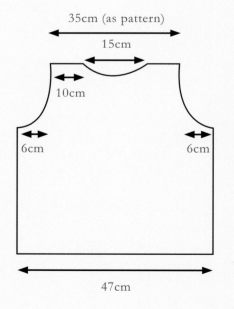

ALTERING ARMHOLE DROP

This is quite a simple alteration to do: all Rowan patterns ask you to work straight until the armhole measures a specific length, so you simple reduce or increase this to the amount required.

What you do need to think about is the sleeve that fits into the armhole: see Altering A Sleeve Head (see page 70).

ALTERING THE SHAPE OF A BODY PIECE

There are two aspects to altering body shaping: altering an already fully fitted garment, and changing a straight garment to a shaped garment to suit body shape, which is what we are looking at here.

It may be the case that you don't need to just tweak a body size; you need to change the shape of the body completely. The example we're looking at on page 76 is taken from page 61; it was the conclusion of looking at how your measurements compared to a pattern.

The width at the lower edge of the jacket matches what you need, but the measurement

at the underarm is different, making the shape you actually want to knit quite different. (For many years I knitted for a friend who loved this shape – she had large hips but her bust and shoulders were quite narrow. I can still see her face when she tried on the first sweater I made her; she was so pleased to have a garment that didn't make her look wide from top to bottom, and it took pounds off her.)

In this example the lower edge measurement is 47cm and you need to get to 43cm for the bust. You have 44cm in which to achieve all of the decreases.

1 Calculate the tension over 1cm: in this instance 2 sts and 2.8 rows.

2 Calculate your measurements into stitches:
47cm x 2 sts = 94 sts
43cm x 2 sts = 86 sts
44cm x 2.8 rows = 124 rows

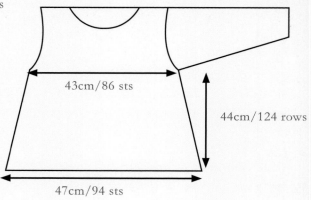

43cm/86 sts

44cm/124 rows

47cm/94 sts

3 You now need to calculate how many decreases you need to do by subtracting the number of bust stitches (86) from the lower edge number of stitches (94), giving 8 sts to be decreased. You decrease on both sides, so 4 decreases need to be made in the 124 rows.

4 Now divide the 124 rows by the amount of decreases: 124 ÷ 4 = 31. So you need to decrease every 30th row. This is a subtle decrease; yours may be more dramatic than this, but the theory is the same.

Turn to page 65 to read about things to consider when altering shape and adding stitches to a patterned garment.

MAKING ALTERATIONS TO A SHAPED GARMENT

In the line drawing below the garment is fully shaped and the correct measurements are key for this garment to look great and, importantly, feel great. As previously discussed (see page 21), it is important to know the overall length of your body and the length from the nape of your neck to your waist. We will work through two examples; one to alter the length, and one to alter the width.

The theory is the same for increasing and decreasing, so don't worry if what we discuss here is in fact the opposite of what you want to achieve.

ALTERING THE OVERALL BODY LENGTH OF A SHAPED GARMENT

1 Calculate the tension over 1cm: in this instance 2 sts and 2.8 rows.

2 In this example the garment needs to be longer, but measurement A is correct, so the lengthening should take place at measurement D. We'll say that D is currently 11cm and needs to be 14cm, so 3cm extra.

3 Work this out as a number of rows: 3cm x 2.8 rows = 8.4 rows (round down, so add 8 rows).

4 So we have to go from 84 sts (E) to 76 sts (F) in 40 rows (D + 8 rows). That's 8 stitches to be lost, and we decrease at each end of the row, so 4 decreases. Divide the 40 rows by 4 decreases to know that you must decrease every 10th row.

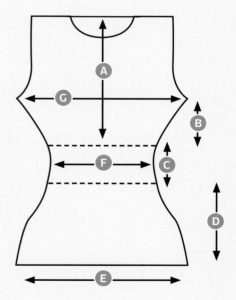

A = 39 cm (110 rows)
B = 18 cm (50 rows)
C = 6 cm (16 rows)
D = 11 cm (32 rows)
E = 42 cm (84 stitches)
F = 38 cm (76 stitches)
G = 42 cm (84 stitches)

Altering the Upper Body Length of a Shaped Garment

If you need to alter length A, you would have to change measurement B following the steps on page 77.

If you require the same overall length but need length A to be longer, you would need to increase measurement B, but decrease measurement D by the same amount.

Altering the Width of a Shaped Garment

1 In this example, measurement E needs to be wider by 3cm, but the length is fine. E is currently 42cm and needs to be 45cm.

2 Calculate how many extra stitches are needed to add 3cm by multiplying the measurement by 2 stitches, to give 6 stitches extra needed.

3 If you need the 3cm extra throughout the garment, then you can keep all of the shapings exactly the same but just remember to add the 6 sts on when the pattern tells you how many stitches you should have after completing a section of shaping.

4 It may be that you need the extra 3cm at measurements E and F, but not at G. So you would need to calculate the increases differently between F and G.

For example, at F you have 82 stitches (76 plus extra 6), and you need to get to 86 stitches (the pattern's measurements) over the 50 rows of measurement B. So that is just 4 stitches over 50 rows rather than the 10 stitches the pattern gives.

5 You will increase at both ends of the row, so instead of working all of the increases the pattern says, you will divide the 50 rows by 2 increases to know that you need to decrease every 25 rows. In this example I would probably increase at row 23 and then at 46 (rather than on rows 25 and 50) so the final increase wasn't at the last shaping point.

Once you have mastered these examples you can calculate any shape you need. To help you understand and practice the process, work out the stitches, rows, increases and decreases needed to turn these measured shapes into knitting instructions.

The answers are on page 96, try and do it yourself before looking at them. (Just a tip: remember the shaping is only on one side here.) Good luck!

EXERCISE 1

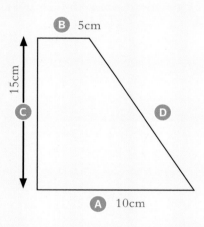

The tension is 20 sts and 28 rows to 10cm.

EXERCISE 2

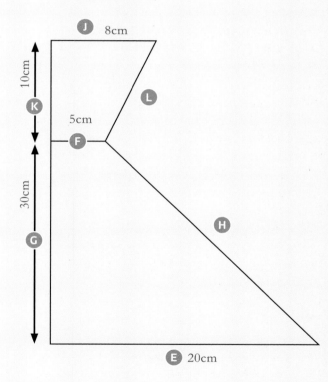

NECKLINES

With all my experience of helping people choose which design to make, I am never surprised to hear: 'I love the sweater, but the neckline wouldn't suit me'.

You have to break it down and decide exactly what it is you don't like: is it the width of the neck, is it too open? Or is it too high at the neck, or too low? If you have a large bust it is better to show your neck than hide it under the sweater, so maybe you need to turn a high crew neck into a more flattering V-neck. Whatever the problem, it is easy to alter.

When we looked at measuring garments (see page 36) I asked you to check the back neck width and the depth of the neck; hopefully you did this for all the necklines you like. If you are unsure, go back and try on a garment and make sure you are happy with the fit of the neck, because now is the chance to get it right. It is a good exercise to measure lots of flattering garments in your wardrobe and see if there is a similarity in neck measurements, even though the shapes seem different.

The neck fit comes from the measurement of the back of the neck (which on average is 14–15cm), then measure the drop of the neck: measure straight down, don't follow the curve of the neckline. Measure down from your shoulder until you are level with the bottom of the neck: an average drop measurement for a crew neck is 8cm.

Sometimes it isn't the drop or the width of the neck that puts you off, but simply the shape the neckband is. Is it a polo neck and you don't like anything that high? Or is it a crew neck and you would prefer a turtle neck? In these instances you keep the same measurements for the neck, but alter the actual neckband.

If it is the case that the neck is too wide or narrow, then you will need to make some alterations. This example is a boat neckline, which is quite hard to wear: I'll show you how to change it to a crew neck shape, which can then easily become a polo or turtle neck.

The tension here is 24 sts and 29 rows to 10cm, and the pattern tells me that the width of the back neck is 44 sts.

1. Calculate the tension over 1cm: in this instance 2.4 sts and 2.9 rows.

2. Convert the width to centimetres by dividing the 44 sts by 2.4 sts to give 18cm.

3. The back neck width required is 14cm: 14 x 2.4 sts = 37 sts.

4 The drop neck measurement required
is 8cm: 8cm x 2.9 rows = 23 rows. The
new neck drop is plotted on the graph
paper. At the base of the neck there
is normally a plateau, which is usually
calculated as being a third of the back
neck width. In this instance, 37 stitches
divided by 3 will give 12 stitches on
the plateau.

5 Draw in the new neckline with a curved
line, and then plot the individual
decreases, as shown here, making them
symmetrical (if a symmetrical neckline
is what you want).

Making changes like these will raise the
question of how many stitches to pick up for
the neckband or the front bands: don't worry,
this is covered in the next chapter.

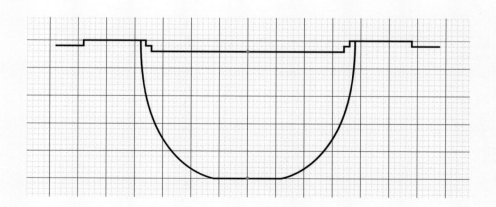

CHAPTER 6

TECHNIQUES AND BLOCKS

When the hard work of the calculations has been put into practice and all the knitting is completed, you are at the final stage of putting the pieces together, and possibly picking up stitches for the neck or front bands. And all too often people rush this bit: they so want to try on the completed garment that they neglect a couple of simple but essential techniques that can make a big difference to the look, and fit, of it.

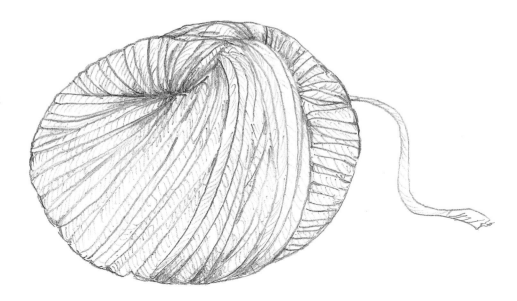

BLOCKING

This is a technique so often skipped, and yet one that is so important to the look and feel of your garment.

If you do quite a bit of knitting it would be worth making your own blocking board. The main advantage of having a blocking board is that when you have blocked something it is best left for a while pinned out, so you can simply move the board to somewhere out of the way rather than having to leave the ironing board up (which is what most people use as an alternative to a blocking board). Another advantage is that a blocking board covered with checked fabric – such as gingham – makes it really easy to ensure the garment pieces are pinned out straight and even.

TO MAKE A BLOCKING BOARD YOU NEED

A piece of chipboard to the size you wish to make the board. (You need to be able to pin out a back and front together.)
Some wadding to cover the board; this needs to be fairly thick.
A piece of gingham fabric to cover the board and wrap over the edges.
A staple gun to attach the wadding and fabric to the board.

Simply lay the wadding on the board, wrap it over the edges, and staple it to back of the board. Then lay the gingham fabric over the wadding and staple that to the back of the board, ensuring the fabric is straight and pulled tight. You now have a surface you can slide pins into at an angle in order to pin out knitting.

TO BLOCK A PIECE OF KNITTING

Lay out the knitted piece without stretching it and pin it to the blocking board all the way around the edges. It is very easy to over-stretch the fabric and when you have then steamed it, it becomes too large. Ensure that the piece is lying flat and is squared up to the checks of the fabric as appropriate, and that elements are in the right position; for example, the armholes are at the same depth. It is always worth checking the measurements before you complete the pinning and begin the steaming process.

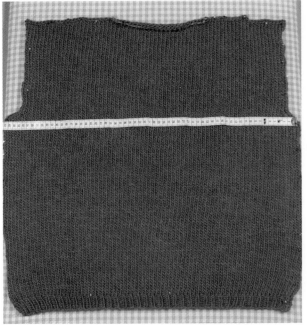

Now you can begin steaming. How you do this depends on the fabric you have pinned out. If it is pure cotton then you can have your iron on full steam and fairly hot.

For pure wool and wool-blend yarns, bring the steam setting down to a medium heat. If the yarn is particularly fine, then cover the pieces with a thin piece of linen fabric.

Hold the iron or steamer above the knitted pieces and do not place the iron directly onto the fabric at all. Steam the knitted fabric, then allow it to dry and cool before removing the pins.

If the yarn is a non-iron fibre, such as 100% acrylic or angora, then you need to cold-block it. Instead of using an iron or steamer, fill a clean water spray bottle – as used for indoor plants – and mist the pinned-out piece with water. Then cover it with a towel and pat dry. Allow to dry before removing the pins.

When you have completed all the seams, press the garment again, using a cloth to protect the fibre.

PICKING UP STITCHES

When I came to write this part of *Knit To Fit* I had to think about what you would specifically need to know to deal with any alterations you'd made to a pattern. I realised that if you have altered the length of a cardigan, you would then not know how many stitches to pick up for the front bands; if you have altered a neckline the same problem would occur.

All the other finishing techniques would remain the same, and as we are pressed for space in this book, I will leave you to read one of the other good books on finishing techniques that are already available.

HOW MANY STITCHES TO PICK UP

I know some people struggle with this, even if they haven't altered the pattern. The key is to know the calculus the designers use so you can work it out for yourself.

Basically, you need to pick up three consecutive stitches, miss one, then pick up the next two consecutive stitches, then miss one; repeat this sequence right along the edge being picked up from. This will give you an even picked-up edge without it frilling out or pulling too tight.

If you feel you have to pick up where you should miss one because it will leave a hole, then pick it up, but remember to knit it together with the next stitch on the way back across the first full row,

When working front bands of a cardigan, I find it best to pick up along the front edge and work the band on the side. The band lies much better than knitting up the front, and this method also makes it easier to calculate where to place the buttonholes.

Placing the buttonholes is something you must take into account when altering the length of something: pick up the button band first, then, when you know how many stitches you have, plan the buttonhole positions on a piece of paper.

1 When starting to pick up stitches I tend to go under the first edge stitch and then wrap the yarn around the needle and bring it through. You can take just half of the edge stitch, but for a neater finish it is best to take the whole edge stitch.

2 Now pick up three consecutive stitches.

3 Miss the next stitch (which is actually a row as you are working sideways), and then pick up the next two consecutive stitches

4 Continue in this way along the edge to create a neat, evenly spaced edging.

I find it is always worth working bands and necks on a circular needle. When you have picked up all the stitches along the edge, you can then stretch the circular needle out and you will be able to check that the edge is lying flat and even.

On pages 87–94 you will find blank body blocks that you can photocopy and annotate with your measurements. All the basic shapes (see pages 36–43) are here, and you should add to them so that they more accurately reflect the garment you want to knit. So if, for example, you want to knit a fitted V-neck cardigan, then photocopy body block 4 (see page 90), and draw on the right shape neck and a centre front line. Alternatively you can trace off these blocks and make amendments to your tracings. I have not put arrows onto these blocks as you will want to measure different elements and pre-drawn arrows will just become confusing.

On page 95 you will find a blank version of the record card that is filled out on page 45. Do try and keep a record for every project you knit: it's both good practice and genuinely very useful.

BODY BLOCK 1

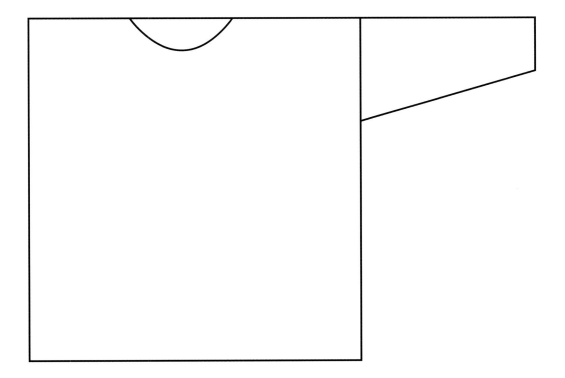

BODY BLOCK 2

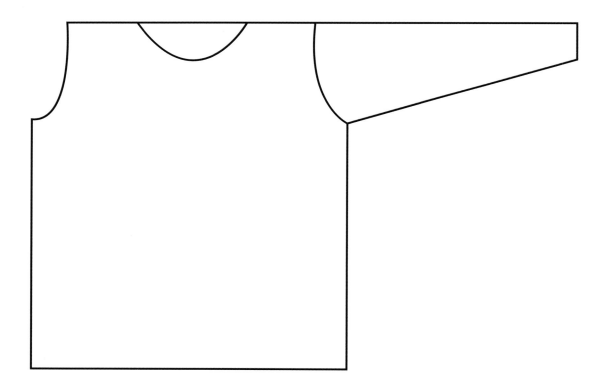

BODY BLOCK 3

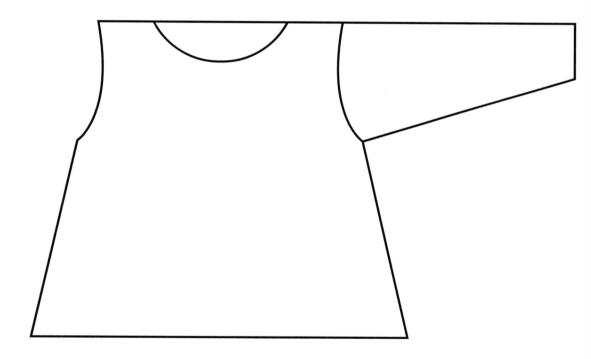

BODY BLOCK 4

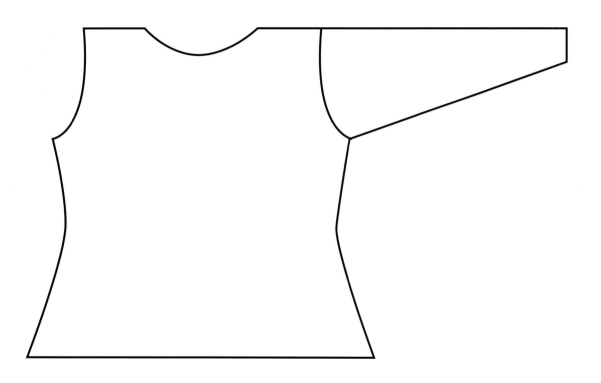

BODY BLOCK 5

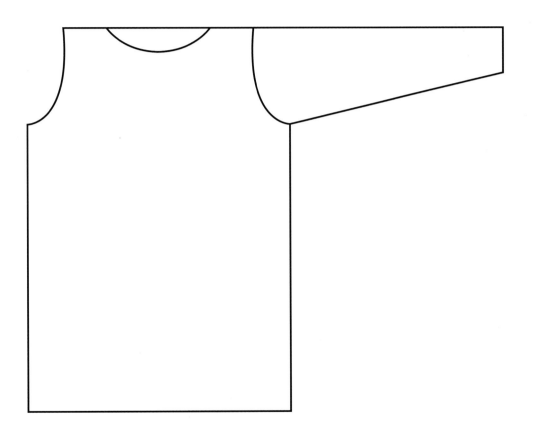

BODY BLOCK 6

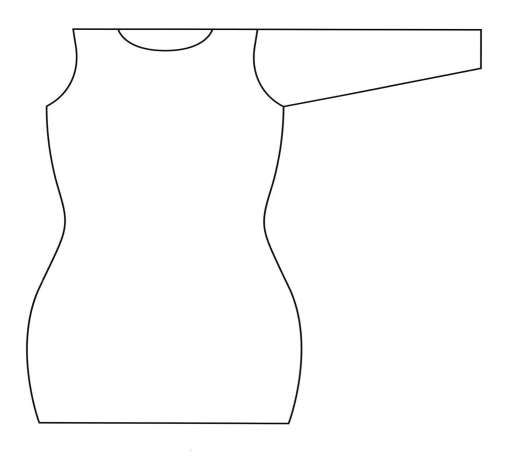

BODY BLOCK 7

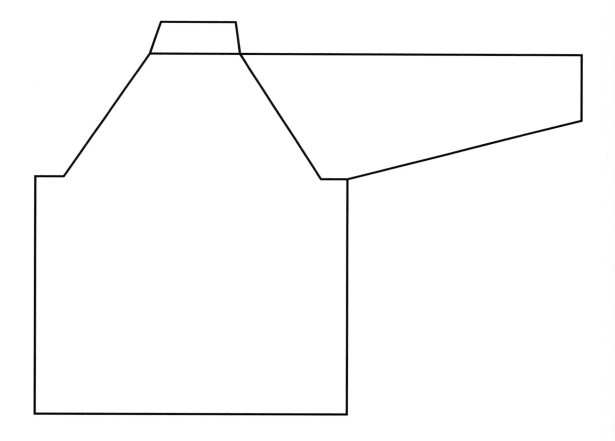

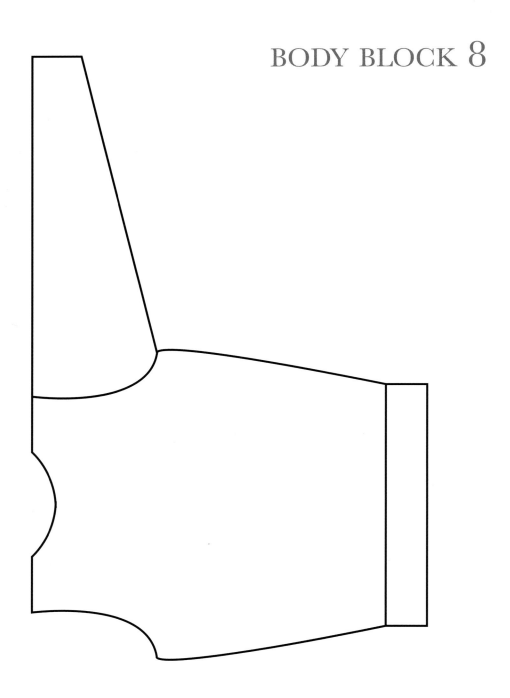

Project Record Card

Name of project: Alterations to pattern:

Source of pattern:

Yarn used (name/brand/
colour/fibre content):

Tension:

Needle Size:

Key Measurements:

ANSWERS TO THE EXERCISES ON PAGE 79

Exercise 1
A - 20 sts
B - 10 sts
C - 42 rows
D - 4.2 rows (increase every 4th row)

Exercise 2
E - 40 sts
F - 10 sts
G - 84 rows
H - 2.8 rows (decrease every 3rd row)
J - 16 sts
K - 28 rows
L - 4.6 rows (increase every 5th row)

Well, here we are at the end of the book. I do hope I have helped you gain the confidence to ensure you have the correct measurements for your body shape, and that you have the finished items that you enjoy wearing. Knitting is a fabulous pastime and knitwear is great to have as it can be individual and special to you. And now hopefully your knitwear shows your body to its best and feels fantastic!

Happy Knitting!

Sharon x

ACKNOWLEDGEMENTS

I would like to thank everybody that has helped me pull this book together. First of all my wonderful son, Darren, for making my vision come to life in the book. Kate Haxell for her patience and attention to detail, as always; without her I wouldn't of been able to achieve it with my Coats work schedule. And a huge thank you to both of them for their patience waiting for me to read and check things!

As always a special thanks goes to Kate Buller at Rowan for supporting my ideas, and to David Macleod and the team for all the information we needed in order to show the examples at their best, and for his enthusiasm for the project.

Finally, a special thank you to the wonderful illustrator, Lauren Bishop for bringing our basic ideas to life in a captivating way.